To Vita!

Eugene Rodrigue

BIRD OF FOUR HUNDRED VOICES

Vive la Culture!

BIRD OF FOUR HUNDRED VOICES

A MEXICAN AMERICAN MEMOIR OF MUSIC AND BELONGING

EUGENE RODRIGUEZ

HEYDAY
50
Berkeley, California

All song lyrics composed by Eugene Rodriguez and published by Los Cenzontles Publishing; except "The Dreamer," composed by Jackson Browne and Eugene Rodriguez and published by Los Cenzontles Publishing and Swallow Turn Music; "El Corrido de Cecilia Rios," composed by Los Cenzontles and Gilberto Gutierrez Silva; verse for "Pajaro Carpintero," composed by Gilberto Gutierrez Silva; verses for "El Fandanguito" and "El Siquisirí," Public Domain; "Red River Valley," Public Domain; and the pandemic decima, composed by Verenice Velazquez.

Library of Congress Cataloging-in-Publication Data

Names: Rodriguez, Eugene, 1962- author.
Title: Bird of four hundred voices : a memoir / Eugene Rodriguez.
Description: Berkeley, California : Heyday, 2024.
Identifiers: LCCN 2023058550 (print) | LCCN 2023058551 (ebook) | ISBN 9781597146449 (hardcover) | ISBN 9781597146456 (epub)
Subjects: LCSH: Rodriguez, Eugene, 1962- | Guitarists--United States--Biography. | Cenzontles (Musical group) | Popular music--United States--History and criticism. | Folk music--Mexico--History and criticism. | Mexican Americans--Music--History and criticism. | LCGFT: Autobiographies.
Classification: LCC ML419.R605 A3 2024 (print) | LCC ML419.R605 (ebook) | DDC 787.87092 [B]--dc23/eng/20240126
LC record available at https://lccn.loc.gov/2023058550
LC ebook record available at https://lccn.loc.gov/2023058551

Cover Art: David Flury
Cover Design: Archie Ferguson
Interior Design/Typesetting: theBookDesigners

Published by Heyday
P.O. Box 9145, Berkeley, California 94709
(510) 549-3564
heydaybooks.com

Printed in East Peoria, Illinois, by Versa Press, Inc.

10   9   8   7   6   5   4   3   2   1

To Milo

LOS CENZONTLES

A nonprofit cultural arts academy, a band, a production studio, and a community space for youth and families, working together to amplify our Mexican roots in the Bay Area and beyond.

The Songs of
BIRD OF FOUR HUNDRED VOICES

Los Cenzontles
With...

Jackson Browne, The Chieftains, Ry Cooder, David Hidalgo, Flaco Jimenez, Taj Mahal, La Marisoul, Raul Malo, Linda Ronstadt, Daniel Valdez, y muchos más.

To hear the songs mentioned in the book, scan this code:

To learn more about Los Cenzontles
Please visit **loscenzontles.com**

CONTENTS

•••

1 El Vuelo del Cenzontle 1

2 Family Roots 11

3 Wings and Covenants. 25

4 Artist in Residence 41

5 Fandango 47

6 Papa's Dream, Los Lobos, and Lalo Guerrero 63

7 Joy and Uncertainty in a Changing Neighborhood 69

8 Space 79

9 Pasajero, a Journey of Time and Memory 87

10 The Pedagogy of Intangible Heritage 101

11 A Garden, Not a Flower Store 119

12 David Hidalgo 131

13 Crossing Cultural Rivers 141

14 State of Shame 155

15 Linda Ronstadt 175

16 Songs for Strange Times 191

17 Regeneration 203

Acknowledgments 211

About the Author 213

A Note on Type 215

CHAPTER 1

●●●

EL VUELO DEL CENZONTLE

In the spring of 1994, I arrived at the San Francisco Airport from Southern California, where I had been producing the children's album *Papa's Dream* with Chicano folk rockers Los Lobos. I stopped abruptly at a newsstand, struck by the front page of the *San Francisco Chronicle*, which showed a photo of a group of crying Mexican American teenagers. Those were troubled years on the streets of our East Bay neighborhood, and I understood that Latino youth appearing so prominently in the press could only mean that someone had been killed. Looking more closely at the photo, I recognized one of the teens as Ruth Arroyo, a member of the youth music and dance group I was directing. Alongside her friends, she was mourning fifteen-year-old Cecilia Rios, who had been raped and murdered on her walk home from Richmond High School.

The teens were struggling not only with grief but with the fear of violent retaliation, based on rumors—amplified by the press—that Cecy's murder was gang related. While local news sensationalized the story as yet another tragedy from the barrio, our young people struggled to make sense of it. The tattered walls of local buildings and schools now included graffiti reading "RIP Cecy," and teens wore caps and T-shirts with the same, along with her photo. Eventually, her murder was found to be unrelated to gangs, but painful emotions remained, and many went unexpressed. I wanted to do something to help. Sensing that the Mexican cultural traditions we were teaching our students could somehow be of service, we invited the teens to write verses about their friend.

They would write in the form of a corrido, a narrative ballad of heroism and tragedy made famous during the Mexican Revolution (1910–20) and still popular in our community. I felt that chronicling the events of Cecy's death would be less emotionally intrusive than having the teens write directly about their feelings. So, in a group, they began to tell her story, and began to express themselves, some for the first time.

There were people who advised me against doing this project because they felt that it reinforced a negative image of our community, but I knew it was important, so I insisted, and the teens agreed. The story was true and their grief was real. I set the verses to music, and the members of Los Cenzontles recorded "El Corrido de Cecilia Rios" at a local home studio. The boys played trumpets, vihuelas, guitars, and guitarrón, and the girls, including Ruth, sang the verses. The corrido became a valued remembrance for them and the community, and it remains a poignant example of the healing power of culture.

EL CORRIDO DE
CECILIA RIOS

Aquí me pongo a cantar
Versos de una triste historia
Que la llevo en la memoria
Imposible de olvidar

Siempre fue Cecilia Rios
Alegre y muy compañera
Apreciada por donde quiera
No andaba metida en líos

Buena hija fue en su casa
La amaban padres y hermanos
Los amigos, los paisanos
Era reina entre la raza

Rodeada de tanto amor
Ya por cosas del destino
Fue muy corto su camino
Para tan hermosa flor

Siendo una quinceañera
Le tocó la mala suerte
Pues le echaba la muerte
En una forma traicionera

En el tercer mes del año
El día catorce corría
Un criminal desvaría
Y decide hacerle daño

Recién de México vino
A visitar a su gente
Pero ya traía en mente
El espíritu asesino

EL CORRIDO DE
CECILIA RIOS

Here I will sing
Verses of a sad story
That I carry in my memory
Impossible to forget

Cecilia Rios was always happy
A good friend
Appreciated everywhere
She kept out of trouble

At home she was a good daughter
Loved by her parents and siblings
To her friends and countrymen
She was a queen among Raza

Surrounded by so much love
And by destiny
Her road was short
For such a beautiful flower

Only fifteen years old
Bad luck struck
Death stalked her
Treacherously

It was the year's third month
On the fourteenth day
A raving criminal
Decided to do her harm

Recently arrived from Mexico
To visit his people
His mind already carried
A murderous spirit

La siete daba el reloj	The clock struck seven
La noche venía cayendo	And night fell
Cuando a su casa iba yendo	As she walked home
Miguel Chávez la siguió	Miguel Chavez followed

"Que solo quería robarla,"	"I only wanted to rob her,"
Dicen que les declaró	They say he declared
Pero también la ultrajó	But he raped her
Y terminó por matarla	And finished by killing her

En la escuela Downer fue	It was at Downer School
Donde aconteció el sucio	Where this occurred
Y hoy el asesino preso	And now the murderer lives imprisoned
Vive sin gloria y sin fe	Without glory or faith

Richmond de luto quedó	Richmond was in mourning
Y Cecy al cielo se fue	And Cecy went to heaven
Yo en estos versos conté	Today in these verses
La desgracia que pasó	I sing of the disgrace that occurred

Vuela cenzontle cantor	Fly, singing mockingbird,
Tus trinos serán testigo	Your song will be a testament
Que a Cecy padres y amigos	That, for Cecy, her parents and friends
La recuerdan con amor	Will remember her with love

In the months between Cecilia's death and the recording of her corrido, our youth group, which had begun five years earlier under an artist residency, had transitioned into an independent nonprofit organization. I had named the group Los Cenzontles (pronounced *Los Senn-sont-less*), after a poem I had stumbled upon in 1990. Composed in ancient Nahuatl, it reads:

I love the song of the cenzontle,
Bird of four hundred voices.
I love the scent of flowers and the color of jade.
But more than anything, I love my fellow man.
—Nezahualcóyotl, fifteenth-century poet and ruler of Texcoco

The poem resonated with me because of its touching declaration of love for our fellow human beings, a sentiment that captures the essence of our work. I also loved the Native word "cenzontle" for its sound and look, as well as for the dignity that it affords the remarkable multivoiced bird. The word's English translation, mockingbird, is actually a misnomer, since the bird doesn't disparage what it hears. Rather, it listens to the sounds around it and incorporates them into its own voice—something humans also do innately when we engage with each other. This is culture, which is not just the artifacts that we create, sell, and buy, but the constant, multidimensional process of exchange that shapes who we are as individuals, communities, and societies. There is no more powerful human force than culture, which drives history and defines our lives.

In 1984, I was a twenty-two-year-old music student when I began teaching guitar in a blighted neighborhood in Richmond, part of San Francisco's East Bay. The area, once home to World War II shipyards that drew diverse communities from across America, was home to people who were Black, Latino, Creole, Asian, and white, and the many mixes between them. At that time, my Latino students were predominantly English speakers, born in the United States, who had an arm's-length relationship to their ancestral heritage. In 1989, I began an artist residency alongside a folklórico dance teacher, and together, in an effort to teach Mexico's artistic traditions to community youth, we formed a music and dance youth group that would eventually become Los Cenzontles.

By the mid-1990s, our neighborhood, like many across the country, was transforming due to a historic influx of Mexican immigrants who came to the United States seeking work in the wake of the North American Free Trade Agreement (NAFTA), which had radically reorganized Mexico's economy and incentivized migration. Almost overnight, the majority of our students were foreign-born Spanish speakers. Their families shared cramped living quarters while the parents worked long hours, revitalized the local economy, supported their communities back home, and created opportunity for themselves and their children, forever altering their destinies and identities, and our country.

The arrival of the newcomers expanded the dimensions of our work in every way; the cultural revitalization that I sought from our study of folklore was now on full display within the community. The streets of Richmond resonated with the sounds of not only hip-hop but also mariachi, Norteño accordion, and brass bandas blasting from cars and trucks. The new residents, mostly from small Mexican pueblos and ranches, worked and partied hard, celebrating with large family events, often including live music. Where many Americans saw their presence as a threat in need of containment, I saw it as an opportunity to enrich the cultural fabric and values of our society, which individualism was driving to a lonely, nihilistic extreme. These family-oriented new-comers had strong work ethics and a sense of gratitude, faith, and hope, all sorely needed in our country.

Of course there were social tensions. The sheer numbers of immigrants suddenly arriving in our neighborhood challenged the already under-resourced Mexican American community most directly, exacerbating conflicts between Mexican-born and US-born youth, roughly along North and South gang lines. Few of the teens were actual gang members—the divide was more cultural—but the tensions had serious consequences nonethe-less. Our cultural arts program, based on shared heritage, proved to be a powerful tool for social reconciliation.

In response to the growing need for cultural activities in the community, we became an independent nonprofit in 1994 and moved from Richmond to the adjacent city of San Pablo. Los Cenzontles was then able to deepen and expand our work, and we immediately became a magnet for youth who saw us as a welcoming safe haven from the dangerous streets. During our first week of classes, we enrolled almost two hundred students, mostly teens who were not being reached by other organizations. Los Cenzontles was not the typical generic youth program, where kids were given busywork and treated as if they were nameless and faceless. We had created a place for them that was both challenging and fun, and where their participation mattered. Our festivals, which our students performed at and helped organize, attracted thousands, and our recordings drew listeners from well beyond our neighborhood. It was clear that our distinctive approach was the key to our success, and I knew that, in order to expand this work, we would need to uphold the criteria and deeper values that guided us. With this in mind, we started training our own faculty, staff, and artists from within the ranks of our students.

Today, Los Cenzontles Cultural Arts Academy is run by people who grew up within our program, and it remains carefully structured to provide a safe, stimulating space for children and adults to take the kinds of risks necessary for deep learning, cooperation, and expression. We have trained generations of community youth in traditional Mexican music, dance, and folk arts; we have performed nationally and internationally; we have revived lost traditions; and we have produced dozens of musical albums and documentaries, and hundreds of music videos.

On the walls of our academy, now located in a strip mall storefront, are photographs of our travels, folk masters, musical collaborators, album covers, and generations of students who have considered Los Cenzontles their second home. Though it may seem counterintuitive, our secret of unlocking the power of tradition has challenged how many *see* tradition, and it has even been iconoclastic, pushing beyond the pageantry and chauvinism typical of folk arts programming. In doing so, we have achieved what many people never considered possible, or even important. But massive global changes of recent decades have validated the need to reimagine the way we regard tradition in our lives. The rural communities that once bore and nurtured Mexico's traditions have been forever altered by economic shifts and mass migration, forcing us to reevaluate how we understand belonging and identity.

Thirty-five years after the founding of the youth group, our students are once again mostly US-born, largely the children of landscapers, construction workers, cooks, and domestic workers who immigrated in the 1990s and 2000s. In some senses, our community demographic has come full circle. But, in the process, Mexican immigration has also irrevocably transformed, and strengthened, our neighborhood and country. And yet, even though people of Mexican origins have been here for centuries, we are still considered by many as outsiders. The work of Los Cenzontles affirms, and insists, that we not only belong but are equal stewards of this, our country.

The underlying mission of Los Cenzontles is simple: local artists training local children in community culture, something that every neighborhood should have. But simple solutions are often difficult to realize and sustain in a world complicated by bias and inequity. To fund our work, I am constantly having to convince people of the value of the Mexican American community and the relevance of cultural arts, butting up against the deep misconceptions concerning social class, race, ethnicity, and identity that are so tightly woven into America's myths they can seem impossible to untangle. But for over thirty years we have found ways to thrive, thanks to persistence, focus, luck, and the hard work and sacrifices of our local young people, otherwise dismissed by society, who run the organization, and the many wonderful artists and supporters who have joined our journey.

I view my work with Los Cenzontles as an exploration of self as well as a contribution to our country and world. Like many Mexican Americans, I was raised with a sense of obligation and responsibility, which I pass on to my students in the hopes that, someday, we will all be regarded as mutual stewards of our society and planet. My lifetime and career has coincided with the historic browning of America, but recently, just as I felt that we were making progress toward a more just society, the resurgence of white supremacy brutally interrupted my sense of optimism. However, I continue to believe that our best path forward is to be visible and to affirm our right to be ourselves. In a representational, multicultural democracy, cultural engagement is as important as voting. Bigots who understand the power of culture use it as a weapon for darkness, so we must use culture to assert a vision of light.

CHAPTER 2

●◗●

FAMILY ROOTS

At first glance, little about my childhood would have foretold that I would dedicate my life to Mexican folk culture. I am a third-generation Mexican American who grew up speaking English in a middle-class neighborhood in Southern California. Unlike other children and grandchildren of immigrants who distance themselves from their raw ancestral traditions as they acculturate, there was for me something in the unvarnished immediacy of roots music that gave me a sense of connection and possibility.

Both sides of my family quickly climbed the socioeconomic ladder through work, education, and intermarriage, which the United States makes possible. My Mexican-born paternal grandmother, Enriqueta Guillen, used to warn her daughters against marrying Mexican men, and of her eight children—Manuel, Raul, Alma, Robert, Norma, Gloria, Fernando, and

Marie—only her first two sons had children with Mexicans. My parents, Manuel and Emilie, had three sons—Phillip, Eugene, and Gregory—all dark-skinned. For my immediate family, culture, both its outward display and its effect on our inner lives, was an ever-present force.

My father, Manuel H. Rodriguez, born in 1930, spoke only Spanish when he entered kindergarten, a circumstance for which the teacher nuns scolded my grandmother. From that moment through the rest of his childhood, she ensured that he spoke only English. Seeking personal reconciliation, he later studied Spanish and worked as a Spanish teacher at Los Angeles Valley College until his retirement four decades later. He lived in the LA area his entire life and was a formal, highly educated man with a love of books and a strong sense of obligation. As a young man, he was offered a Rhodes scholarship, but he refused it, since, being the eldest son, he felt a greater responsibility to earn money for his mother and siblings. He later earned a law degree, but when he realized he didn't like being a lawyer (and wasn't primarily driven by status), he returned to teaching, which he loved.

My father considered culture a powerful force in life, not just as a marker for social advancement but as a way to help us understand the fullness of who we are—a lens whose focus shifts as we navigate different periods of our lives. During our visits throughout my adulthood, we spent hours talking about family and culture, and he was candid about his emotions and discoveries, mindful that he was providing me with an example of self-reflection. He once confided that he consciously decided to appreciate Mexican ranchera music in spite of it being the soundtrack to his father's drunken abuse in their chaotic home. He felt that he had to separate the actions of his father from the music in order to fully accept himself.

My mother, Emilie Cacho, the daughter of farmers, grew up in Chula Vista, California, not far from the Mexican border. Like my father, she was poor as a child, and in her younger years she helped her parents by working in the packing shed, memories of which caused her pain even in old age. In a childhood made heavy by toil, she remembers times when hearing live music in her home created moments of lightness. Her father, Antonio Cacho, took her mother, Herminia Farias, from her family's impoverished ranch in Michoacán in the 1920s, when she was only fifteen years old. Her brothers, angry to lose their only female sibling (who performed the domestic duties), shot at the couple as they left, killing the dog that accompanied them. I recently found out that when my grandfather returned years later, his brothers-in-law took their revenge by ambushing and shooting him. This time they did not miss, but he survived. My grandmother didn't return to her place of birth for thirty years and had no nostalgia for Mexico. The United States provided my grandparents the opportunity to grow their farming business, which eventually became successful. They sent their five daughters—Rosa, Petra, Emilie, Irene, and Delia—to universities, and their two sons—Luis and Tony—remained nearby to work in agriculture. Eventually, my grandmother hired her brothers as laborers.

Resentment can fester in families for generations. My Grandpa Cacho, who was orphaned as a child and forced to work for another family under conditions that my mother described as akin to slavery, was hardworking, motivated, and focused on bettering his lot and that of his children, but unfortunately his demanding narcissism cast a shadow on his descendants that endures to this day. I did not know him well, as he and my grandmother were separated for as long as I can remember. His thoroughly Mexican manner of dressing, complete with cowboy hat, impressed upon me that we were from different worlds. Perhaps to bridge that gap he once gave me a cancionero, a book of popular Mexican songs. A few years later I sent him a recording of my guitar playing, but his only reply, made to my mother, was to complain that it did not include any of the songs from his gift of years before. He could see me only as a reflection of himself.

After their children became adults, my grandfather left my grandmother to start another family in Tijuana, a betrayal for which some of his children never forgave him. In the 1970s he lost most of his money in the Mexican peso devaluation, while my grandma remained in Chula Vista with her money intact. But she had never stopped loving him. At his funeral in the early 1980s, his two families gathered around his open casket, hardly acknowledging each other. I remember being surprised at how small his body was compared to his outsized impact on our family.

My parents met at UCLA in the 1950s, when there were only a handful of Mexican American students. My mother was pretty and my father was handsome; it may have been inevitable that they would marry and start a family. In 1966, when I was four years old, they moved us out of our South San Gabriel neighborhood, which was becoming unsafe, and into a house kitty-corner from my aunt and uncle—my father's sister Alma

Gregory, Emilie, Phillip, Manuel, and Eugene Rodriguez

and her husband, Roland Sarlot—who had built a house in the picturesque foothills of middle-class Glendale. Our new place was a large, beautiful Spanish-style home built in the 1920s, with a red-tiled roof, balconies, and a yard with four olive trees big enough for us children to climb on and play freely around. We were one of the few Mexican families in the neighborhood.

For my parents, parsing issues of language, class, and educational status added to the typical stressors faced by all married couples. They read books on child rearing and discussed how they would raise me and my brothers, intent on providing us more stability, support, and space than they had had. They were eventually unable to keep their marriage, but when I was young, our family appeared picture-perfect: "a typical, middle-class, child-centric, Mexican American family," as my father once described us. English was our language, except for times when my parents spoke in Spanish to keep their conversations private—my mother in her family Spanish, and my father in his school-taught Spanish, which was itself an occasional point of tension.

My father always remembered how his Mexican aunts, who had criticized him for not speaking Spanish as a boy, never complimented him for relearning it as a young man. He concluded that people will always find a way to feel superior to others. I have come to believe that language and identity are intensely personal choices that are not to be judged by others at all. My wife, Marie-Astrid, and I would later teach our son Emiliano to speak only English—not Spanish, not French (her native language), and not Vietnamese, the language of her father. Our priority was that he learn to communicate well in his first language and then he could decide for himself later if he would learn a second, or third, language, as did my wife, my father, and I.

When I was growing up, my parents encouraged me and my brothers to embrace the many cultures that made up our lives, and to defend our right to have complex identities; they were both independent-minded, and we became the same. Like most Mexican Americans, their musical tastes were varied. Their record collection included albums by Louis Armstrong, Javier Solís, Vivaldi, Rodrigo, Herb Alpert and the Tijuana Brass, Billie Holiday, Glenn Miller, and Eydie Gormé and Los Panchos. Our walls had prints by Diego Rivera, El Greco, and Van Gogh, as well as still lifes painted by my mother, who took art classes for a time.

Emilie and Manuel Rodriguez

My earliest memories of music are of my father singing us cowboy songs such as "Red River Valley" and "Home on the Range," music that he heard as a young man working at the Downtown Los Angeles post office alongside Dust Bowl immigrants from Oklahoma. He once told me that he chose these types of songs to reinforce our sense of American identity. And although he sang and played guitar with little finesse, the tender affection that he expressed imprinted in me a deep connection between music and love. Hearing him sing "Wayfaring Stranger" never failed to make me cry. Sometimes hearing the song still does.

He regularly took us to the Griffith Park planetarium, the Huntington Library, LA's Natural History Museum, and the La Brea Tar Pits. Always playful with language, he referred to our armpits as tar pits, and it was only later that I learned this was not the actual term. We toured all of California's historic missions and took two road trips to Mexico City. History was important to him, and he wanted us to know that we were part of it. In his later years, he worked on our family genealogy before there were online services to assist, convinced that knowledge about family heritage could enhance our lives in practical ways. His intention was not to romanticize our family histories but, rather, to understand them, recognizing that blind allegiance to family can be as hazardous as ignoring it.

When we were young, my mother was fully attentive to us, cooking complete meals nightly. She made tacos with ground beef, chicken cacciatore, chorizo and eggs, lasagna, homemade flour tortillas, and tamales at Christmastime. We always had plenty of fresh vegetables and fruit. In the summer she served us cantaloupes, honeydew melons, and watermelon, which she cut into pieces and removed the seeds from. My cousins Charlie and Richard, from Chula Vista, occasionally brought us crates of cucumbers that they grew. We ate them whole, peeled and salted. And on those special nights when my parents went out and left us with a babysitter, I was thrilled to eat TV dinners in my pajamas.

My mother threw big birthday parties for us, with piñatas and trays of her enchiladas, inviting our many cousins and neighborhood friends. Her brother Louie would sometimes bring to family parties the mariachis that he led. He sang beautifully and played various instruments, including guitar, vihuela, guitarrón, and trumpet. My uncle Tony sometimes played vihuela, and my aunt Rosa, who had a lovely, refined voice, would sing a few rancheras or boleros. When she and Louie were young children, my grandfather used to take them to Tijuana to sing duets on early-morning radio. After a while, she began declining our requests to sing, making me believe that something had tarnished her joy for music making. While I missed hearing her, it was fortunate that my aunt Delia, the youngest of my mother's siblings, had a strong voice and big personality for singing rancheras.

As I got older, I joined in on guitar. Rancheras, with their simple 3/4 and 2/4 rhythms, were not a problem, but the sones, which use complex 6/8 rhythms, were a challenge to strum, and the boleros had fancy, fast-changing chords that I had trouble grasping. My uncle Louie lacked the patience or interest for breaking them down for me, preferring instead to show off his own virtuosity. He once told me that I could not be a mariachi because I was not born in Mexico (though neither was he). At those same parties, my brother Phillip and I played pop songs in English. Phillip had a gifted voice and charming personality, and his theatrical renditions thoroughly entertained the family. I was his accompanist, a role I have often played with many others throughout my life.

I cherished the warmth of my Grandma Cacho, whose house in Chula Vista was still surrounded by farmland when I was a child. I am told she was one of few people I allowed to hold me as a baby. She was a reserved, dark-skinned woman with a quiet, wicked sense of humor. Once, when I was a teen, she drove me out to a field in her Cadillac to find a pig to eat for a family party. Standing in front of the animal, she gave me a handgun and told me to shoot it in the head. Knowing full well that I was a city boy incapable of the act, she laughed with her hand over her mouth. Typically, she spoke to me in Spanish. I spoke to her in English. In that relationship, I learned that culture was many things beyond language and place of birth. The smell of fertile soil, the taste of home-cooked food, and the sounds of music all formed me, as did her hugs and mischievous laughter.

My parents encouraged us to be creative and communicative. When I was four, my father began to record me and Phillip, then seven, telling jokes and doing interviews as make-believe characters. Phil, my first collaborator, and I continued to record ourselves throughout our childhoods. I invented voices for made-up characters—including Freddy F. Freddy and Baby

Grandma Herminia Cacho and Eugene

Junior—and would joke around and tell stories to Phil. Our first musical duo was called the Kabuki Band, in which we banged on pots and pans and blew a hair dryer as instruments. We eventually graduated to taking guitar lessons at Charles Music, the local music store, when I was eight and he was eleven. Our first teacher, Hank Bood, was a serious, bald German man who wore dark turtlenecks and had little patience for our pranks. When he asked Phil to remove chewing gum from his mouth one day, Phil stuck it onto our music stand. We kids thought it was hilarious. Mr. Bood did not.

We also spent our time making homemade smoke bombs, blowing up Hot Wheels cars, producing circuses for our families, and playing questionable practical jokes on friends and cousins. At the age of four or five, my cousin Roland and I almost burned down my house. We'd shoved a push broom into our open furnace so that its flaming bristles could light dried twigs, serving as candles, on a birthday cake we had fashioned from mud. When we were about ten we formed the Mini Magicians duo and performed magic shows for our family. We even did a few paid gigs for children's parties. On one occasion, I improperly set up the finger guillotine trick and smashed the finger of our child volunteer, making him cry. I believe that may have ended my career in magic. Roland, however, continued to work at it and eventually became a professional magician.

Many of my childhood pranks masked the fact that I was a worrier, and my active imagination often amplified those worries into negative fantasies. My father taught night classes twice a week, and on the occasions when he arrived later than expected, I would fear for his safety, feeling a sense of dread that would crescendo until I heard the reassuring sound of the door latch, followed by his signature whistle. To this day, the emptiness of time invites worry and anxiety, so I try to stay busy with ideas, activities, and the reassurance of human contact.

In the mid-1970s, my parents' marriage began to disintegrate, with increasing arguments, angry silences, and unexplained absences. Despite their intelligence and many refinements, they were unable to sort through their emotional distress without creating a theater of chaos. Our home no longer centered around us children but around adult pain, and I learned to be on constant alert for signs of trouble, which began with a heavy feeling in my gut. Our family was breaking, and its pride and privacy were betrayed by the spectacle and intrusion of a public divorce.

At that same time, the suffocating Los Angeles smog, which was also at a crisis point, felt like an outward manifestation of the anxiety that polluted my mind and spirit. On those days in which smog alerts were declared, my lungs stung with every breath. And at night the sky was covered by a dome of haze and city light that shrouded the stars, dulling my sense of possibility and menacing my sense of well-being.

Through this time I clung even more closely to television. Cartoons, sitcoms, and old movies provided me with a comforting sense of escape and wonder. I loved macabre movies like

1963's *The Raven* with Vincent Price and Boris Karloff (based on the Edgar Allan Poe story), classic mysteries like Basil Rathbone's Sherlock Holmes films, and trickster programs like black-and-white reruns of *Candid Camera*. In the ninth grade, I joined my junior high school's theater program. The teacher, Sherry Stockhammer, recognizing either my talent or my emotional need, placed me in every lead role for that year's plays. I was Black Bart in the cowboy Western, Boston Benny in the 1940s gangster play, and Santa Claus in the Christmas show, a casting choice that must have been somewhat provocative in white, conservative Glendale, California, of the 1970s.

At the library, I borrowed tapes of 1930s and 1940s radio comedies, which I then transcribed to practice and perform. One of them was "Who's on First?" by Abbott and Costello, a routine I performed with my friend Tom Denton. At fourteen years old, we were selected to appear on *The Gong Show*, the subversive television talent show in which the worst acts were "gonged" away by the panel of three celebrity judges. When my father took me and Tom out of school to go to the TV studio, our classmates gave us a heroes' send-off.

An entire week of episodes was taped in one day, so we waited for our turn in a large room surrounded by weirdos, exhibitionists, and professionals seeking exposure. We performed our bit pretty well, giving me hope that we might win. We did not win, though neither were we gonged. The host, Chuck Barris, remarked on my "smile of confidence" and nearly pinched my cheek, and one of my favorite performers, pie-in-the-face comedian Soupy Sales, rated us a 10 out of 10, saying, "We comedians have to stick together." Another judge, jazz singer Sarah Vaughan, whose legend I was still unaware of, gave us a 10 as well. It was Jaye P. Morgan, whose talents I did not know (and still don't), who gave us a 9, dashing our hopes of winning the first prize of $516.32. A lounge act wearing bell-bottoms won with the song

"Ease on Down the Road," from *The Wiz*, fronted by a Black man singing alongside a redheaded white woman, a pairing that was still a novelty in 1976. As our consolation prize, we got an electric wok and a set of sheets, which we gave to our mothers, and we were immortalized by our classmates.

During the later part of the 1970s, which seemed to me to be the decade of divorce in America, my extended family also grew further apart. D.j.s, not mariachis, now provided music for family parties that were held in hotel conference rooms instead of on the farmlands around my grandma's house, which had been converted to the Don Luis Mobile Estates, named after my uncle Louie and inhabited by grouchy old women. It is typical for immigrant families to steadily grow apart, but moving away from a collective structure didn't diminish family resentment. After my grandma died, in 1994, one of my mother's siblings, angry that their mother had left equal shares of her considerable estate to all of her seven children, drew a gun at an estate meeting, demanding that they receive the lion's share for having remained in the family business. A majority cowered and acquiesced.

My parents reinvented themselves after their divorce. Following years of working as a teacher, my mother earned her master's degree in marriage and family counseling. My father continued to learn languages, travel, and read. Both enjoyed cheering on their sons as we built our careers, Phillip as a filmmaker and Gregory, who is four years younger than me, as a writer. In time, I pursued music out of a need to recreate a lost sense of wholeness and family unity (either real or imagined), since, in my hazy childhood memories, that wholeness centered around music making. My search for how I fit into the world became my career.

When I was a teenager I began studying classical guitar at the music store with Tom Runyan, who introduced me to styles that allowed me to explore a more serious side of my nature. I especially loved playing the dark, romantic Spanish repertoire of

Tárrega and Albéniz, for which I had an aptitude. My first public performance was a recital at Glendale's Brand Library, a local monument noted for its distinguished arabesque architecture. I also showed off during lunch in the quad of Glendale High School, which provided me a certain status among my peers. Years later I ran into Mr. Runyan, who had become a therapist and had since heard from my mother about my parents' divorce. When I thanked him for his guidance, he marveled that he had not been aware of my family troubles while they were occurring. To be sure, at that time I was not interested in putting my personal pain on display. Music was my way to escape it.

Eugene at fourteen years old, 1976. Photo by Owen "Mac" Haggerty

At fifteen I had an experience that changed my life. I was alone in my bedroom, looking out the window at an unusually clear sky. I remember becoming overwhelmed by a sense of connection to everything, free from anxiety and worry. I felt at peace, as if I were enveloped by God. The moment did not last long, and I soon returned to myself, but the memory of the experience remained in my mind as a beacon of hope during times of uncertainty. It taught me that I must trust that I am part of something bigger than myself, and that connection is the ultimate goal, even if I must go through separation and pain to get there.

CHAPTER 3

●◗●

WINGS AND COVENANTS

When I was growing up, there were few Mexican Americans on mainstream television or on the radio or in the movies. Popular culture taught us that Anglo men drove and stewarded our country and culture. When *we* appeared in popular media, we were villains, buffoons, or cowards, usually played by white actors with darkened skin. The reason that we could not represent ourselves, we were told, was that there was not enough talent in our community. So, in addition to being marginalized, we were also taught to bear the responsibility for our own disenfranchisement.

We learn to distinguish between our American and Mexican identities when we are young because we are forced to choose between them. As kids, my brother Phillip and I often debated how much of our identities were formed in our Mexican families versus how much were formed by white Glendale. We never settled on a conclusion. In retrospect, I would say that we were formed mostly by our families, while taking full advantage of the privileges of growing up in a safe, fully resourced, entitled neighborhood.

Of the hundreds of online videos that I have produced for Los Cenzontles, the one that attracts the most vitriol is one in which we ask Mexican American elementary school students, the children of farm laborers in wealthy West Marin County, whether they are more Mexican or American. The children, who understand that the question is about cultural differences, respond with clever, playful insight. But the video itself continues to receive a barrage of comments that viciously question the children's allegiance to either the United States or Mexico, and the commenters also scoff at the legitimacy of the very question, which, for us, is essential. That the innocent expression of youth can provoke such controversy demonstrates how violently America's myths of purity are enforced, how stubbornly American diversity is denied, how Mexican Americans are so easily viewed as illegitimate, and what our children must contend with simply by being themselves.

When I was in school, overt ethnic insults were relatively rare, perhaps because there weren't enough of us to present a threat. More commonly, white schoolmates would tell me that I didn't "seem like a Mexican," and it did not occur to them that they were saying something offensive. On the contrary, they thought it was a compliment. In those days, cowboy shows and movies distinguished between the elite light-skinned Spanish dons and the dark and dirty Mexican bandidos. Of course, the conniving dons were not as altruistic as the Anglo pioneers, but at least they were clean.

A few years ago I received a social media message from a childhood classmate who was going through a twelve-step program and needed to make amends to the people he felt he had wronged. He reminded me that he had once called me a "dirty

Mexican" in elementary school. I had told my mom, who told *his* mom. After his mom punished him, she then revealed that he, too, was a dirty Mexican.

Our elementary school had a morning flag patrol composed of boys who marched in military formation chanting, "Left, right, left . . . left . . . ," until they reached the school's flagpole and ceremoniously raised the American and California flags. Most days, old neighborhood men, many of whom must have been World War I veterans, stood on the school's perimeter and saluted. One afternoon my brother Phillip, who was on the patrol that day, asked my father what the Alamo was. When my dad asked him why he was asking, Phil replied that one of the old men, seeing him, had yelled out, "Remember the Alamo!" My father was livid.

My parents vigorously defended themselves, and us, from being stereotyped, and their example taught us to do the same. We learned to think critically and argue—a privilege in America normally granted only to white men. Dark-skinned Latinos, in contrast, are expected to present ourselves as unthreatening by acting either childlike or saintly in order to advance in our careers. If we are strategic, we are considered sneaky. If we are assertive, we are branded as angry. It is not a coincidence that the model men of color held up by this nation—Cesar Chavez, Martin Luther King Jr., and Mohandas Gandhi—were all pacifists. There are few things that white Americans fear more than Black and Brown rage, though recent events prove that white rage is our nation's true threat.

I also learned to dodge stereotypes by unabashedly embracing my eclectic tastes and interests, and rejecting any notion that I should confine myself to a narrowed identity. In high school I was not part of any particular clique but was friendly with various groups. To this day, I am the same.

When I was a kid, I enjoyed the righteous revenge film *Billy Jack* (1971), in which a "half-breed" white and Native American ex-Marine (played by a white actor) uses martial arts to protect a group of Native students, taught by a white hippie woman, from racist rednecks. The scene where a young Native boy is tormented and humiliated by bullies in an ice cream store was almost too painful for me to watch, as he was the only character in the film who I resembled. Only Billy Jack's powerful, lightning-fast feet could save the boy as he cowered there, impotent and paralyzed. This was not who I wanted to be, but I knew it was how many others expected me to be.

While in high school I worked as a bag boy at the Alpha Beta grocery store. I was so highly motivated and attentive that I was quickly promoted to checker, something rare for someone my age. One afternoon, a white customer refused to allow me to check his groceries because I was Mexican. As mine was the only checkstand open at that moment, the manager told me to step aside while he tended to the man, something my parents, had they been there, would not have allowed to happen. The experience left me feeling humiliated and vulnerable.

Only recently did I learn that up until the late 1960s Glendale was a "sundown" town, meaning African Americans were not welcome within city limits after dark. It had also been the West Coast headquarters of the American Nazi Party as far back as the 1920s. I have wanted to believe that Glendale's racism has since been neatly tucked into the past, but I have learned through social media that many of my classmates have joined today's embittered right wing. Instead of being grateful for the privileges of their youth, they resent the notion that children of color might enjoy the same today.

●●●

UC Santa Cruz was the only college I applied to. I was attracted to its focus on the liberal arts, as well as to its beautiful campus on a cattle-speckled hill overlooking Monterey Bay, which was entering a pattern of wet weather in 1980. Walking to class over wooden bridges, surrounded by towering redwood trees in the rainy mist, couldn't have been more different from the semi-arid brown hills of Glendale. The change in my surroundings made me feel that I could distinguish myself in this new place. I was not only breathing a different kind of air, through which, on clear nights, the stars sparkled, but I was surrounded by a different kind of culture, one that, for a while, nourished my growing sense of independence. On certain days, under steely blue skies, I rode my motorcycle through the forested backcountry, ending up at beaches in isolated coves accessible only by hiking through artichoke fields.

Even while I was in college, I had no idea what I would do for a living, nor did I worry about it. My interests didn't add up to any marketable skills, but I enjoyed learning. I took music, poetry, literature, and easy "science for poets" classes. Perhaps I was always destined to create my own career, although I would not have known it then. To this day, I advise young people to take their time deciding on a major while enjoying the process of education in order to develop a feeling for where their interests and aptitudes meet.

My parents did not pressure me to choose a career, nor did they criticize my choices. They were busy with their own lives, which was among their biggest gifts to me. Throughout my teens and early twenties, I was burdened with a debilitating sense of worry for their well-being, as the trauma of their divorce weighed heavily on me. So when they continued to grow into new lives, it felt like they were giving me permission to move on with mine.

The social bubble of Santa Cruz in 1980 was an extension of the hippie era: politically liberal and white-centric. There I would learn about a different kind of discrimination from what I'd experienced in Glendale. Insidious and condescending, it was the kind that tolerates and celebrates you as long as you conform to who they think you should be. I was beginning to open my eyes to the world and gradually learning to distinguish what was real.

At UCSC, I took an ethnomusicology class and participated in the student mariachi, led by a professor who taught us standard mariachi techniques and repertory, and how to stand like "real Mexicans." Although not Latino himself, he appeared to identify so completely with a host of macho stereotypes that he seemed to think he was more Mexican than his Mexican students. In those classes, I was happy to learn the strums and chords that my uncle had been too impatient to teach me, but, while I was still too young to fully articulate these thoughts at the time, I knew that I needed to avoid people like that professor going forward.

During those years, I also discovered how some of my fellow Latino students judged each other's ethnic authenticity based on where we grew up, what languages we spoke, what accent we had, and who we dated. I didn't feel that I had anything to prove to them *or* learn from them, so I stayed away from those kinds of people too.

Since I had enjoyed acting in junior high, I took a drama class one year at UC Santa Cruz. The teacher, who was highly skilled, taught us the basics of body movement, for which we were required to wear tights. Being from a modest family and still coming out of my shell, I didn't feel ready to expose myself in that way, and my classmates' exhibitionism made me uncomfortable. On an overnight field trip to Ukiah, we slept in yurts and some of the students took hallucinogens and ran around naked, mistaking debauchery for creativity. It was all very decadent, which I found so repulsive that I decided I'd had enough of drama class.

I have always loved music, but once I began to take higher-level music theory classes, my joy of music education screeched to a halt. As a young adult, a great many subjects confused me, and I felt left out of many conversations, including, for instance, ones about politics and sports. I can begin to understand a subject only when I have the time and space to unravel and process its layers. Music theory classes presented a barrage of complex concepts that confused me, making me feel less, not more, connected to music. Instead of finding the emotional outlet that I sought, I found only frustration and stress. On top of that, I felt out of place socially. I took a songwriting class dedicated to pop music, but it was taught by a jazz fusion musician and dominated by a clique of hip kids who were constantly showing off their knowledge of chords with extended harmonies, while I was there to learn the simpler harmonies of pop music, as the class title implied. One day a student began talking about "mojo," a word I was unfamiliar with. Intimidated, I didn't ask what it meant, which was for the best. After another student asked, one of the hip kids sneered, "If you have to ask what it means, you don't have it." The teacher smirked as the insiders all laughed smugly. I realized I did not belong there. So, in the middle of the second quarter of my third year at UCSC, while struggling to complete a musical analysis of a Mozart piano concerto in music theory class, my anxiety reached a climax and I quit.

After living on campus for two years, I had moved into the upstairs flat of a Victorian house on Maple Street in downtown Santa Cruz with my former dorm mate Michael Drinkard. It had big wood-framed windows that let in generous amounts of sunlight and the bay breeze. Its bare furnishings included only the essentials needed by young people in transition. My large room, which contained a futon, a lamp, a chair, and a music stand, had double glass doors that opened to the living room, which was usually filled with music, either live or on the stereo. Michael, a writer, and I enjoyed a rich friendship of imaginative conversations and midnight walks to the Santa Cruz beach. We turned our neighbors into characters and invented elaborate storylines to go along with them. Michael was easygoing and attentive, giving me the space to stretch myself and explore the world with confidence. It was important for me to be accepted and appreciated for who I was during this time when it felt like so many others were pressuring me to be somebody else.

At this point, I was part of a music group called Ahora Sí with fellow UCSC students Guillermo "Willie" Anderson, from Honduras, and bassist Pablo Aslan, from Argentina. At our Maple Street house, we held rehearsals for which I cooked black beans and rice. We focused on nueva canción, a genre of politically conscious songs born of the 1960s and '70s social movements in Latin America. The songs of Atahualpa Yupanqui, Victor Jara, Silvio Rodríguez, Pablo Milanés, and Violeta Parra opened my heart to their messages of empathy. Their melodies, chords, and rhythms were a new and welcome challenge for me. This was a time when US intervention in the war in El Salvador was activating Americans to form solidarity committees and host events, several of which we played for, including our largest, with Mexican singer-songwriter Gabino Palomares.

Ahora Sí: Pablo Aslan, Guillermo Anderson, and Eugene Rodriguez, 1982. Photo by Michael Drinkard

We also played tropical songs and boleros that I had heard on José Feliciano recordings. His renditions of classics like "Nosotros," which my aunt Rosa used to sing with my uncle Louie, did not conform to rigid stylization but rather, to my ear, were liberated by his soulful voice and varied musical influences, such as blues and rock. His covers of English-language hits like "Light My Fire" and "California Dreamin'" are far more interesting and soulful than the originals. I recently heard him perform in Oakland, and while at first it struck me that he was now a man in his mid-seventies, made frail by time, I was startled by the power of his voice, which brought a tear to my eye and reminded me of his extraordinary cultural and artistic influence on me and our culture. In 1968, his heartfelt Latin rendition of "The Star-Spangled Banner" at a World Series game was met with a racist backlash that almost destroyed his career, but he had persevered and proved that it is possible, and powerful, to be all of who we are.

●●●

In 1982, Marie-Astrid Do moved into the smallest room of our three-room flat, having arrived from France with her family three years earlier, at the age of twenty. She had come to Santa Cruz to work at a French bakery making pastries with the skills that she had learned at the famed Cordon Bleu in Paris. The daughter of an Alsatian mother and a Vietnamese father, she was graceful and beautiful, and still is. Because she is French, many people assumed she led a privileged life, but she was raised working-class and within an educational system that demanded conformity at the expense of creativity—a troubling situation for someone as highly creative as she. Nor was it easy growing up mixed-race in France. People were often rude to her mother for having mixed children, and the French government would not issue Marie-Astrid a passport to take school trips across the border to Germany because of her father's place of birth.

Marie-Astrid and I did not date during the brief time that we were housemates, nor did we spend much time together. It was only after she had moved out of Maple Street to live in a greenhouse that we rediscovered each other on a local bus and began dating. For two people with no money in Santa Cruz, our dates were very informal, focused mostly on getting to know one another, especially since we had already experienced each other's banalities, having shared the same closet and bathroom as housemates. She was mysterious to me then, and in many ways she still is, as we are very different. Perhaps that is what we were looking for, and what has sustained us. Quiet and introspective by nature, with perceptions that often surprise me, she follows her creativity without measure and fiercely defends it from convention. In 1983, we moved to a small in-law and began the life of a couple.

Eugene and Marie-Astrid, 1984. Photo by Michael Drinkard

During that time, I was playing solo classical guitar in restaurants and decided to take lessons again. I remembered seeing a guitarist named David Tanenbaum a few years before whose emotive and physical performance made a strong impression on me. I looked him up and asked if I could study privately with him, and he agreed. Every two weeks, I took a Greyhound bus from Santa Cruz to Oakland where he lived. It felt like a pilgrimage on which I was to finally get the musical education I needed. He taught me from a place of knowledge, practicality, and concern, focusing on the intricacies of guitar technique and the Baroque repertory of Bach and Scarlatti, as well as certain contemporary composers. He lent me records and books, and we discussed a broad range of topics that connected music to worlds of ideas, as instrumental technique means nothing if you have nothing to say. I practiced for hours a day with intense dedication, and at some point David suggested that I apply to the San Francisco Conservatory of Music, where he taught. I did and was accepted. In 1984, Marie-Astrid and I moved to San Francisco.

The Conservatory was more performance oriented than UC Santa Cruz, which was a positive for me, but I found most of my classes to be an interruption of my private studies with David, which now took place in tiny, sterile practice rooms within rigid time slots. My education was no longer an expansive exploration but a narrow tunnel aimed toward juried recitals and graduation. I continued to play increasingly demanding repertory, but I never had the time to develop a nuanced relationship with the music. The process was joyless, and the only exhilaration I felt was a mix of fear and relief. Even my interactions with the other students were largely meaningless distractions.

To make money, I taught guitar lessons and performed community outreach gigs, some of which ranged from the bizarre to the otherworldly. I once performed for a group of elderly Asian women at a community facility in Chinatown, and in the middle of one of my pieces, the entire group stood up and walked out without comment. I was later told that it was the hour of their favorite Chinese soap opera, but no one had bothered to mention that beforehand. On another occasion, I was hired to play at a Mensa-type meeting of eccentric overweight men in the living room of a Victorian in the Lower Haight. Once my set was finished, a group of young men scantily clad in leather arrived to perform theirs.

I was anxious to graduate as early as possible, as my student debt was mounting, so after completing my bachelor's degree in guitar performance, I earned my master's in one year and graduated in December 1987, the same month that Marie-Astrid and I married. Because of my parents' divorce-related tension, we had canceled the large family wedding we had planned and instead wed on our own at a bed-and-breakfast in Mendocino. The old VW van of the friend who was officiating our ceremony broke down on his drive up, so instead of getting married on Saturday, December 12, we did so on Sunday, December 13, witnessed by the bed-and-breakfast owners and their cat. Marie-Astrid wore a dress her mother had created for her.

When we married, Marie-Astrid was pregnant with our first child. A month later, we noticed a lump on her clavicle, which was diagnosed as stage 4 Hodgkin's disease, a type of cancer of the lymph nodes. She was twenty-eight and I was twenty-five. It is difficult for me to describe my worry and fear; the news threw me into a tailspin. The day that we learned by phone of the initial diagnosis, I had a gig playing solo background music at the home of a wealthy San Francisco doctor. I brought Marie-Astrid with me because I could not bear the thought of leaving her home alone. She was, of course, well dressed and lovely as always, but the doctor was clearly annoyed by her presence, even after I explained our situation. He grudgingly allowed her to remain as long as she stayed alone in a small bedroom with the door closed. It was the last time that I took such a gig.

When we finally were able to meet with her doctors in person, their cheerful demeanor shocked us both. They explained that her particular cancer was 80 percent curable, a statistic not often used when treating cancer. However, it would require a difficult six-month regimen of chemotherapy, followed by months of radiation. Naturally, they wanted to begin her treatment as soon as possible in hopes of stopping the cancer, but they also had to delay in order to give the baby time to develop. It was a precarious situation.

On April 14, seven months into the pregnancy, the doctor induced Ariel's birth, when he was old enough to survive outside the womb. Marie-Astrid's treatment began immediately. The doctors declared our son healthy at birth, but his release home was repeatedly delayed by complications that confounded them, and frightened us. After a series of tests, which alternately raised and dashed our hopes, he was eventually diagnosed with a congenital heart defect, the only remedy for which would be risky

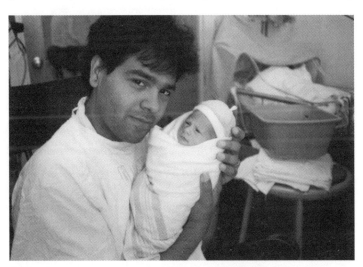

Eugene with Ariel at UCSF Hospital, 1988. Photo by Marie-Astrid Do-Rodriguez

open-heart surgery. Even surrounded by an excellent medical team and supportive family, nothing could allay the deep worry of those excruciating periods of waiting, and all the while I was supposed to be strong for Marie-Astrid while she endured her own fears for our baby along with the horrors of chemotherapy.

We planned to baptize Ariel in the neonatal intensive care unit before his surgery, but the hospital's Irish Catholic priest, Father Mickey, declined our request because Marie-Astrid and I had not been married in the church. However, I learned that we could perform the ceremony ourselves, so with the nurses, our mothers Emilie and France, my brothers Phillip and Gregory, and Marie-Astrid's sister Anne, we did so, with Marie-Astrid wearing her wedding dress, which no one in the family had yet seen. Ariel's baptism taught me that the covenant between people united by love was far more powerful than that of any institution, especially one that could be so cruel to an innocent child and a young couple in pain. Ariel died during surgery on May 14, one month from the day of his birth. At his funeral, Marie-Astrid lost her first hair to chemotherapy.

The year that followed was a crucible of grief, worry, and Marie-Astrid's heroic battle against cancer. On the few occasions when she was hospitalized due to the ravages of chemotherapy, kind nurses allowed me to sleep on a couch in her room. Marie-Astrid sought ways to heal by tapping into her deep wells of strength, and as time progressed, her creativity, which now involved jewelry design and drawing, became a critical act of self-care for her. We both still feel deep gratitude for the doctors, nurses, and social workers at the UCSF Medical Center, and all those who dedicate themselves to healing others.

Meanwhile, I was beginning my professional career with an intense need for consolation and connection but also a pressing need for income. We had little money, few financial prospects, and mounting debt. We lived on food stamps while navigating the indignities of the social services system in order to gain Medi-Cal health coverage. We were more fortunate than many, though, as we had family support. My mother and father visited and sent money. Marie-Astrid's parents hosted us at their home, providing reassurance and meals. My uncle Roland and auntie Alma gifted us a new car and a performance-quality guitar and, after Marie-Astrid was well enough, a belated honeymoon road trip through the Southwestern desert.

Of course, our personal problems did not shield us from the ongoing insult of discrimination. When I applied for a job teaching guitar at a local state university, the blond-ponytailed music chairman felt it necessary to assure me that he supported affirmative action but that *this* job was just too important to be given to someone to meet a quota. Even at the Conservatory, where I was one of the top players in my class, I was subjected to white male students accusing me of receiving scholarships based solely on my ethnicity rather than my talent. I have always been a productive, hard worker who expected only a level playing field, but that makes no difference to the types of people who make these kinds of comments as a way of feeling simultaneously superior to and charitable toward others.

At this point, I decided I could not return to the loneliness of playing solo guitar, and instead I joined up with different musicians and groups and played various styles of music, including nueva canción, Latin fusion, Puerto Rican bomba, American pop standards, and Latin American classical repertory. I learned a lot about music and musicians and was beginning to see how the world operated, by observing both good and bad examples and, of course, by making my share of mistakes. I also met many people whom I would reencounter in meaningful ways through the coming years.

CHAPTER 4

●●●

ARTIST IN RESIDENCE

Back in 1984, I was still a music student when I began teaching guitar at a nonprofit arts organization located at the edge of a blighted area of Richmond in the San Francisco East Bay. Their facility was an ornate three-story structure from the 1920s that had seen better days as a theater and ballroom in its distant past. It had an unkept wooden interior, faded carpets, and old black-velvet curtains that surrounded a pockmarked theater floor. I knew nothing about nonprofit organizations at the time, and during my first years there I saw a few executive directors cycle in and out. Although I never worked more than a handful of hours a week, I considered my BART trips across the bay from San Francisco an adventure and an opportunity. In addition to teaching guitar lessons there, I also produced a classical guitar concert series for the public. I used to dream of finding new spaces within the old building and imagined using its quirky nooks and crannies to launch new projects.

While I was getting to know my young students, I was startled by the poor quality of education that they received in their Richmond schools. The public schools I had attended in Glendale included core academics as well as electives in music, theater, art, shop, drafting, printing, and P.E.—all during school hours. Each class was fully equipped and rigorous, with competent teachers from whom we learned to use our minds and bodies to understand ideas, to make things, and to be creative and resourceful. In contrast, the children in Richmond received little, and little was expected of them. Community advocates who claimed to represent their interests supported lowering educational standards rather than challenging the students and fighting for better schools. My US-born students, whose first language was English, were routinely forced to take English as a Second Language classes taught by unqualified teachers. And many teachers, instead of believing in their students' ability to learn by being challenged, advanced them through the grade levels regardless of educational attainment. In the words of many of my students, school was "a waste of time."

In Richmond, I met many people who made a living by advocating for the "community," a term they mindlessly repeated, with a patronizing tone, to refer to a broadly diverse group of people as if they were a faceless, voiceless monolith. Instead of taking the time to get to know the varied, complex interests within the community, the advocates served mainly their own agendas. It was all performative and wordy, and even the kids made fun of them. Understanding the pernicious effect of this mindset, I did my best to focus on my students as individuals, each with a name, a face, and a story.

During this time, I also gave adult guitar lessons out of our San Francisco apartment, as well as lessons to wealthy children at their homes. I was grateful for the work, but I far preferred teaching the Richmond kids because they regarded their lessons as something essential, which made me feel that I could actually make a difference in their lives. After a few years, I began teaching in the afterschool programs at a handful of elementary schools in Richmond and San Pablo, where I met children who would later become members of Los Cenzontles, some of them for life.

One, Angel Abundez, began as my guitar student at Downer Elementary in 1987, at the age of ten. He was a determined, responsible boy, the eldest of three brothers raised by their single mother, Angelita, in a San Pablo neighborhood where passersby would never consider stopping. In poor communities, there are always scholarship programs that airlift out children who are clearly gifted and socially adaptable, while the rest of the children languish. I knew that Angel, with his intelligence, curiosity, and discipline, was the kind of child who was going to find a way to succeed no matter what. But I also understood that there are drawbacks to being a scholarship child, so my challenge with Angel was to encourage him to have fun while he learned. I did not want *any* child to lose their sense of self as the price of success. Thirty-five years later, Angel is an engineer and a family man living in a large suburban home. He credits me with making him believe in himself and providing him a sense of purpose and pride, but I was simply building on what I could clearly see in him.

I began teaching Hector Espinoza at Richmond's Lincoln Elementary School in 1988, when he was eight. Raised by his grandparents, he was a fragile child whose future seemed less certain than Angel's, and he remembers that his hands used to tremble in fear during our lessons. He later confided that while my strictness intimidated him, it also pushed him past his fear, providing him the confidence and skills to pursue his love of music, a passion that kept him moving forward, and still does. He wove in and out of Los Cenzontles throughout his youth and became a core member of our teen banda in the late nineties. He is still my go-to banda and mariachi arranger for many of our recording projects, and he refers to himself as a "Cenzontle por vida."

After yet another executive director took over the reins at the arts organization, it began to transition into a multicultural center, creating performing groups that represented various cultures of ethnic and racial groups living in the neighborhood. I was invited to create a Mexican music and dance group with folklórico dance teacher Bernice Zuñiga, who had grown up in Richmond. I was happy to support the effort, as it built on relationships with our existing students and coincided with my own exploration of roots music. Bernice was a caring, patient teacher and taught dance steps and choreographies from various Mexican regions. I learned the standard ballet folklórico repertory as best I could from the warbled sounds of cassette tapes that were dubbed, redubbed, and passed between dance groups.

While Bernice and I taught the styles that we knew, I set out to learn even more. Long before the advent of the internet, after which music of all types was easier to track down, I began visiting Bay Area record stores hunting for new and used albums of Mexican folk music. I found wonderful anthologies of traditional music whose rustic sounds satisfied an itch deep within me. Commercial folk music never gave me quite the same thrill, as there was little room to imagine how I and my students might fit in, but scratchy folk music felt like an invitation to be part of a tradition without barriers. What the music lacked in technical virtuosity and polish, it made up for with personality and depth of expression. I did my best to learn from the recordings and then I taught what I could to my students, who were becoming more like collaborators. They were open-minded and energetic, with the capacity to learn quickly and the gift of being too young to feel inhibited by the musical barriers that limited my adult musician friends. I had always enjoyed learning different styles of Latin American popular music, but playing Mexican music felt like coming home.

In 1989, the California Arts Council (CAC), a state agency, granted Bernice and me a three-year artist-in-residence grant to support our work. The CAC directly paid us a monthly stipend and a budget to invite guest artists of our choosing, providing us with a measure of independence.

The grant did not, however, provide a budget for instruments, of which there are many varieties needed to play Mexico's diverse musical traditions. So, I began to search for them on my own. My uncles Louie and Tony donated vihuelas and a guitarrón to play the mariachi music of western Mexico. Amunka Davila, the Guatemalan father of our students Karalua and Ayla, provided us with a large marimba to play the sones of Chiapas, the Mexican state that borders his home country. A San Jose–based folklorist whom I invited as a guest artist taught us to play the son huasteco, or huapango, and sold me a huapanguera and a jarana huasteca from Mexico's Eastern Sierra Madre.

There is a saying that "la cultura cura," or culture cures. While I agree with the premise, I didn't want to present music to my students as medicine. I wanted them to learn with a sense of fun, purpose, and adventure, and not out of obligation. Angel joined the ensemble and accepted the challenge to learn the harp, which he began with minimal instruction. Siblings Benito and Lola Marines excelled on a number of instruments as well as dance. Their mother, Alicia, worked at the arts organization as an after-school program coordinator, and she and her husband, Benito, a custodian at UC Berkeley, and their three children—including the youngest, Amalia—became an anchor family that supported the group during those earliest years, as other families have since. Our founding class of students also included LaNette Vigil and Ruth Arroyo. Sisters Karalua and Ayla Davila commuted from nearby Berkeley along with their family friend Eliza Garcia.

As the students gained music and dance skills, they were increasingly recognized and invited to perform in the area. They, and their families, also bonded with each other. I began to regularly record them using my four-track cassette recorder, which was a valuable learning tool. And the tapes that we manufactured were a source of pride. Our first cassette was released under the long, generic name of the arts organization, but we later changed it to Los Cenzontles, to give the group the distinction of personality that it deserved. Now, armed with a mission that was coming into focus, and with a group of energetic young collaborators, supportive parents, and a deep, rich cultural heritage to explore, we set out to create what was to become my calling.

CHAPTER 5

●❚●

FANDANGO

When I first met the Mexican son jarocho group Mono Blanco in 1989, I had no way to know that, within a few years, our students would travel with them to a remote Indigenous village in the Veracruz jungle, or that we would help them expand their folk revival to the United States. But with them, we were able to bypass the rigid proscenium of commercial folk music, opening up pathways toward many directions.

While searching for instruments our students could use to play the son jarocho—a style of son named for the Jarocho people from the Mexican state of Veracruz, who are of mixed European, Indigenous, and African origins—I was introduced to Willie Ludwig, a local musician. He told me about the musical group Mono Blanco, who made their own instruments, and he said he was planning to bring them to our area. I offered to help find them gigs. This would be the first time that their rural style of son would be presented in the Bay Area. The group's director, Gilberto Gutiérrez Silva, had been leading a folk revival movement in Veracruz since the 1970s, and for him the effort was deeply personal. Gilberto associated the broken home of his childhood with the disintegration of traditional culture in the ranches and pueblos where he was raised. Hearing elders talk about fandangos of the past, within which musicians were respected members of society, ignited his passion for their return.

It took me a while to understand Gilberto's concepts about the fandango because of the density of the subject, and also because my Spanish was spotty. But in time, his ideas came into focus, and I found that they coincided with my own notions about the connections between music and family: that not all music is performance oriented, separating musicians from audiences, and that music can, at its core, be about something as fundamental and holistic as forging and preserving community bonds. Many teachers of folk music see themselves as protecting, not sharing, cultural knowledge. In contrast, the members of Grupo Mono Blanco, who had a much more fluid connection to the tradition, openly shared it with us. With them, I began to find what I was looking for, not just as a music teacher but as a third-generation Mexican American: an approach that allowed us to develop a more direct relationship with our ancestral heritage and that invited us into the tradition as full participants, not just as bystanders, consumers, or eternal students.

●■●

Fandangos—cultural gatherings centered around folk music and dance—flourished throughout Mexico's ranches and pueblos from the eighteenth to the early twentieth century. Musicians surrounded a raised wooden platform called a tarima, upon which people took turns dancing. The events, which could last for days, celebrated any number of occasions, and they were tightly woven into every facet of community life, forming a cultural cradle that nurtures musicians and sustains the tradition. By the mid-twentieth century, fandangos had almost disappeared in Veracruz, as radio, movies, and television replaced live folk music. During the same time, because of its increased presence in films, the son jarocho became popular throughout Mexico and the world, and traditional musicians left their rural homes in Veracruz to eke out a living in cities, further depriving not only their communities of live music but also the local young people of musical mentorship.

Gilberto understood that to truly revive the fandango jarocho, he must reintroduce all aspects of this musical culture, from teaching music, dance, verse composition, and instrument building to organizing fandangos in the countryside, making sure to center his efforts on children, who would be guided by elders. The result had a profound impact in Veracruz, and it also spread to Mexico City. In 1989, Mono Blanco's Bay Area visit would be a critical step toward introducing the fandango across the United States and the world.

At the time of that visit, the group was composed of four master musicians, each of whom sang improvised melodies, played pandero (tambourine) and quijada (a donkey jawbone used as a percussion instrument), and expertly danced percussive zapateado. Gilberto Gutiérrez and young Patricio Hidalgo Belli strummed five-course jaranas of different sizes and tunings, creating brilliant overtones and rhythmic syncopation, while elder Andrés Vega Delfín plucked a mix of melodies and arpeggios on the four-string guitarra de son using a plectrum made of cow horn. The fourth member, Andrés Alfonso Vergara, also an elder, played harp, not with decorative flash but with substance, deftly trading musical themes with the other musicians. Together they wove a powerful, undulating tapestry of sound that captivated my imagination.

Mexican films and recordings of the 1940s and '50s that featured and popularized the son jarocho had a powerful influence on changing the style's sound to be more commercially marketable, linear, and standardized. Compared to the virtuosic speed at which commercial groups often played, Mono Blanco played in a range of tempos and moods. They also accentuated a Caribbean pulse, reinforcing the fact that their region is situated on the Gulf of Mexico, with strong historical and cultural ties to Cuba and New Orleans. Popular media also created a gentrified image of the Jarocho people, caricaturing them as roguish rascals. In Los Cenzontles' 2004 film *Fandango, Searching for the White Monkey*, Gilberto said in an interview, "The good musicians always came from the countryside. They [the record and film producers] would find them and take them away. And the first thing that they did was to try to erase their rural identities, from the way they talked to the way they dressed—putting them in white outfits and shoes and bleaching their teeth. It was like whitewashing our dignity and identity."

Whereas commercial son jarocho groups sang risqué lyrics that matched the cultural stereotype of the Jarocho people as good-hearted scoundrels, the members of Mono Blanco tapped into the ancestral reservoir of folk poetry and improvisation that communicated the breadth of the human experience. Their performances demonstrated that although the rural traditions of Veracruz had been overshadowed by its commercial counterparts, the rural roots were no less refined or valuable, even as the forces of class stigma and marketability had narrowed its image.

In 1990, I invited Gilberto to return to the Bay Area to teach and perform, this time with his younger half-brother Ramón Gutiérrez Hernández, who would later form the group Son de Madera. My students and I had been studying from videos and recordings I had taken of Mono Blanco's 1989 visit, and some of our youngsters had adapted to this new feel and improvisatory style more easily than I had. Benito Marines effortlessly grasped the fluidity of the jarana's complex rhythmic possibilities, which create more of a musical conversation than simply repetitive patterns, and Angel Abundez's harp playing began to blossom now that he had teachers to emulate. I had learned to play the guitarra de son by transcribing my recordings of Andrés Vega's subtle layers of harmonic and melodic patterns, built on a scaffolding of dance rhythms, such as I imagined Baroque-era folk musicians might have done. I then read from my written notation until I had incorporated the patterns into my fingers and memory, and from there, as I began to improvise, I could sense my thought processes transitioning from one side of my brain to the other, a thrilling sensation that also strengthened my creative agility and strategic thinking.

At that time, we began to plan a Los Cenzontles student trip to Veracruz, where we would study for a week in the city of Veracruz and then travel a few hours away to the pueblo of Santiago Tuxtla to participate in fandangos at their annual fiesta. In those days, most cultural study trips to Mexico never left the confines of a formal institution, in which students learned from an academic professor but never meaningfully encountered people from the community. Our visit would be different.

The extraordinary trip was even more poignant because it followed a tragedy within our community. On September 2, 1990, fourteen-year-old Karalua Davila, a Los Cenzontles dancer, died in an automobile accident while returning from a family trip to Guatemala. She was a beautiful girl who loved to dance and laugh, and although her family was surrounded by support, they struggled to deal with the loss. Her younger sister, Ayla, who seemed to find solace in music, joined us on the trip. In July 1991, community members Benito and Alicia Marines drove their motorhome from Richmond to Veracruz with their children, Benito, Lola, and Amalia, along with Angel Abundez, Ruth Arroyo, LaNette Vigil, "Little Elisa" Montiel, and "Big Eliza" Garcia, Karalua's best friend. Ayla, Marie-Astrid, and I flew, as did Eliza's parents, Jose and Jane Garcia. After arriving to the Port of Veracruz, our group boarded two boats on the delta of Río Jamapa at Boca del Río, and Jose Garcia led us in a sacred ritual designed to honor people who had died unexpectedly. Onto the waters near the opening to the Gulf of Mexico, we sprinkled blue cornmeal and set out floating flowers to ensure Karalua's safe passage to the spirit world.

A few days later, we experienced a total solar eclipse while visiting the Veracruz zócalo, the main square where, at night, groups of strolling musicians play for locals and tourists seated in surrounding cafés. During the day, it is a particularly noisy area in which the sounds of business and construction are amplified by the thick tropical air, but as the moon cast its shadow over the earth that afternoon, the sky darkened and it appeared as though night had suddenly fallen, but without the usual festive music. Birds took shelter and ceased their singing. An eerie silence shrouded the plaza until the sun gradually returned.

●●●

For a week, our students attentively studied with Gilberto and Ramón alongside Mono Blanco's student group, Son la Plaga, in the gardens of the Instituto Veracruzano de la Cultura, an eighteenth-century complex that was located in the city's historic center and had once housed a convent, a hospital, and a school of the Our Lady of Bethlehem order. The building's colonial architecture reinforced the timeless sensation that we were immersed in a culture with a rich and complex history. Many traditional son jarocho verses, in fact, tell of mariners who sailed the seas between Spain, Cuba, New Orleans, and beyond.

Pues, a la ela,	So, to the sails
Golpe de mar	The sea blows
Barquito de vela	Sailing ship
Dime, mi bien, para dónde me lleva	Tell me where you are taking me
Si para España o para otra tierra	To Spain, or some other land
O a navegar al mar para afuera	Or to explore the sea beyond

Angel Abundez (center) with José "Cachurín" Palma Valentín (left) and Ramón Gutiérrez Hernández, Santiago Tuxtla, 1991. Photo by Jose Garcia

Even after a week of workshops, we still had little idea what the fandango would be like, and Benito and Alicia, who seemed to have doubts about it, even considered canceling the trip to Santiago Tuxtla two days prior in order to visit other areas. But we convinced them to remain on course, and we all traveled south to the Tuxtlas Mountains, a region of tropical rainforests and savanna grasslands. The multiday fiestas of Santiago Tuxtla celebrated the patron saint of the ancient, picturesque pueblo, and the fandangos, tucked away in a corner adjacent to the large plaza, did not disappoint. They started early in the evening and lasted until near dawn, beginning with a group of local elder campesino musicians playing into a few microphones around a wooden tarima that was five by eight feet and built about one foot high. After a few sones, other community members joined in and the fandango burst open with all the frenetic energy that had built up since the last celebration.

Playing inside a tightly packed mass of musicians of all ages and backgrounds was a remarkable sensory experience. Singers took turns belting out old and new verses, to which others responded euphorically. Dancers took turns on the tarima, either two or four at a time, following social protocols. Sones lasted minutes or hours, depending on the mood of the participants. No one was in charge, and community consensus reigned (although some individuals tend to be more influential than others). At times there were as many as thirty musicians playing together, some of whom came to reunite with old friends, others to find romance.

I remember a moment when a woman descended from a bus of ballet folklórico dancers to join the fandango. As she jumped onto the tarima, she began to flirt theatrically with a local dancer, as is the stage practice. He, however, saw her flirtation as real—this was not theater for him but a social event—and he responded as such, to the point that the woman suddenly became uncomfortable and returned to the bus.

Salgan a bailar, muchachas	Come out to dance, girls
Que la música las llama	The music calls you
Que los músicos que tocan	And the musicians who are playing
Se les va por la mañana	Will leave by morning

Musicians occasionally wandered off to rest or to have a bite or a drink and then returned reenergized. As the evening wore on, the crowd thinned and the music slowed, with darker verses reflecting somber themes and interspersed less frequently by bursts of energy. The fandango ended in the early dawn amidst the cries of roosters.

El cielo se ennegreció	The sky darkened
Ensombreciendo el potrero	Shadowing the hill
El vaquero se alistó	The cowboy readied himself
Porque vendrá el aguacero	Because rain torrents would soon come
Tal y como lo anunció	Just as was announced
El pájaro carpintero	By the carpenter bird

Our students took to the fandango like fish to water, dancing zapateado as naturally and expressively as they did cumbia at home. Benito moved playfully with agility, fluidly mixing traditional steps with contemporary moves, and always engaging fully with his partners. His sister Lola, a strong, bright girl who celebrated her quinceañera during that trip, danced at the fandangos with the exhilaration and stamina of youth, impressing the older campesinos, who took turns inviting her onto the tarima. Even bleeding blisters on her feet could not keep her away. To this day, she still remembers those moments as glowing highlights in her life.

In the street where the motorhome was parked, Los Cenzontles continued to play and dance. One night, a group of neighborhood kids, realizing that we were Americans, came to show us their breakdancing skills. Our kids, in turn, showed off theirs. We were authentic to them. And there, in the middle of a Veracruz neighborhood, was the lesson: We are all authentic without a stage or lectern to distinguish us.

The fandango in Santiago Tuxtla had surpassed my personal and professional expectations. It was culture in full dimension, far from gatekeepers, authenticity brokers, and culture merchants. We were not crammed into an exhibit of multicultural stereotypes but connecting across and through culture. While playing and dancing, we were all different, but one.

Breakdancing in Veracruz, 1991. Photo by Jose Garcia

●■●

When we returned home, I was eager to share our experiences with anyone who would listen. At a California Arts Council conference, I cornered folklorist Barbara Rahm and showed her unedited video footage that Alicia Marines and Marie-Astrid had shot at the fandango. She responded with enthusiasm, encouraged me to continue, and provided me with keywords that I could use in grant proposals to expand our work through our newly formed Fandango Project, an association of myself, Gilberto Gutiérrez, photographer Silvia González de León, and videographer John Melville Bishop. Our goal was to establish and document son jarocho music, dance, and traditional instrument-building workshops at five Bay Area cultural institutions. We were not a nonprofit organization but had a fiscal sponsor through whom we could apply for grants. I applied for five and received all five. Gilberto would spend the next three years in San Francisco.

The Fandango Project at the Exploratorium museum, San Francisco, 1993. Photo by Silvia González de León

In 1993, while planning for another Los Cenzontles trip to Veracruz, I again invited Mono Blanco to the Bay Area to perform around Cinco de Mayo. Each of their visits was an ordeal of visa applications, logistics, and securing gigs—a challenge, since their style of music was still unknown in the states—but I was on a mission and remained persistent. This iteration of the group included seven musicians and dancers from the Veracruz countryside—Gilberto Gutiérrez, Andrés Delfín Vega, Octavio Vega Hernandez, Tacho Utrera Luna, Dalmacio Cobos Utrera, Rubicela Cobos Roque, and Maria Luisa Romero Cobos—and one nonrural member, young César Castro González, a member of Gilberto's student group. The combination of the rural musicians, most of whom had not spent much time outside their region, with our Chicano students, who also mostly only knew their own neighborhood, was powerful and direct, devoid of pretense, hierarchy, and affectation.

During this time, Los Cenzontles was still housed at the community arts organization, and its director appeared increasingly frustrated with our growing independence. The organization had not financially contributed to our 1991 trip to Veracruz, nor had we expected it to. Our students and I had raised funds by playing for tips and donations in the streets and at flea markets, where we also sold our homemade cassette recordings. But for this next trip, the organization actually prohibited us from raising money and instead promised to do so for us. However, a few weeks before the trip, we were handed a check for only a few hundred dollars.

So, with just a little time to pull together travel funds, we returned to busking for change in San Francisco. One foggy afternoon, playing and dancing outside the Palace of Fine Arts, our friend Maria Luisa Colmenarez, a respected folklórico maestra in the South Bay who was part of our Fandango Project, introduced me to her friend Linda, whom she had invited. Not recognizing that her friend Linda was Linda Ronstadt, I opened up about our dire situation. Impressed by our kids, and feeling for our plight, Linda offered to help pay for the trip. We arranged for her to visit Benito and Alicia's home in Richmond, and although we tried to limit attendance to just our students and their families, it felt like the entire neighborhood had shown up. It was a memorable afternoon of music, dance, and barbecue, and the beginning of a long and fruitful friendship with Linda.

●◆●

Our 1993 trip to Pajapan, in the southern part of the state of Veracruz, took cultural engagement to another level. At that time, Pajapan, a Nahuatl village with small thatch-roofed houses, was an hour and a half drive off of the paved highway. For a week, our Chicano teens lived, played, and slept alongside young Popoluca, Nahuatl, and Mestizo children at a rural school site we shared with roaming goats, pigs, and chickens. Each group of young people initially reacted to the other with the shock of encountering the exotic (they were mostly quiet and observant), but when the students began to play and dance, connections flowered. Benito, while discussing how his limited Spanish made it hard to communicate with words, remarked: "I watch how they play. They watch how I play. That's how we start talking to each other." The first night, by the glow of only a few bare light bulbs in a cement courtyard, the kids strummed, danced, and sang together, growing bolder and bolder by the moment. As the days progressed, the kids continued to study and to play music and soccer, while curious villagers gathered at the perimeter of the school site to observe.

Studying son jarocho with Andrés Vega in Pajapan, 1993. Photo by Silvia González de León

The Popoluca are native to the region. The Nahuatl, who came later, were competitors, and today both groups, along with other Indigenous groups, are among the most marginalized and maligned people in Mexico. Many of the children who attended the camp lived in poverty in the hills and walked barefoot. One told us that townspeople mocked him as a "serrano" (akin to the English word "hillbilly") when he visited pueblos, and others said they wanted to learn their native languages but were prohibited. It occurred to me that the Indigenous and Chicano students shared an experience of marginalization that the other Mexican children present had not.

One afternoon, as the young people grew more familiar and confident with each other, Benito offered to give the Mexican boys fade haircuts, which were popular with urban California teens. In the courtyard, surrounded by the others, Mestizo and Indigenous boys lined up for their new look while a boombox blasted Dr. Dre, to which LaNette was teaching hip-hop moves to the Mexican kids. It was a joyful moment of culture flowing in all directions. I was told that the Indigenous boys had been forced to shave their heads when they returned to school in the fall, but I am certain that their memories have lasted much longer than their summer haircuts.

Before going to sleep each night in the boys' dormitory, amidst the night sounds of the Veracruz savanna, one could hear youthful murmuring in four languages before our elder maestro, Andrés Vega, shushed them to sleep. At this camp, music and dance were our common language. My brother Phillip documented the camp on a Hi8 video camera, capturing footage we have used in films over the years. At one moment, while Phillip and I washed ourselves outside with a bucket of water in a field of grass, we laughed to think that we could never have imagined as children that we would be together in this place someday.

Many think of tradition as a fragile relic or a pageant that we must observe from a safe distance so as not to disturb its purity. But culture is much deeper, complex and dynamic, constantly moving through time and change. Today, the village of Pajapan is connected to paved highways; just as the son jarocho was born of human migration and contact, our visit to that camp was part of a much larger movement of people and culture. Nothing is static. And when we try to grasp only the trappings of culture in an effort to harness them, we lose sight of its true, lasting power.

Benito and Esmeralda dancing in Pajapan, 1993. Photo by Silvia González de León

Spreading the seeds of the fandango jarocho in the early days of its introduction to California was not easy, but it was exhilarating because of the challenge and the rush of discovery. And we continued to promote it. Eventually, the fandango began to take root well beyond our neighborhood—something we had hoped for. As the movement grew, the son jarocho groups that sprouted took different approaches to the music than we had, but I maintain the belief that within tradition there is room for everything, and that the roots of culture are strong enough to withstand these changes.

What did bother me, however, was the rise of a new set of culture brokers erecting barriers within the tradition. In 2012, I received a request from a media outlet to comment on a group of musicians that was trying to regulate the practice of the son jarocho in order to thwart a rising young pop group that was integrating elements of the son into their music. In order to not add to the animosity, I did not provide a public response, but I was appalled to see the return of such a destructive vestige of Mexico's colonial history, one best left buried in the past.

I feel truly fortunate to have been part of the movement when it was still an open exchange of friendship and music. In those early years, the members of Mono Blanco did not treat us with formality or act superior to us, as did other maestros, but they instead invited us to play alongside them, a trait I have since noticed is common to the best artists of all genres. They supported us and we supported them, all of us sharing a common, open purpose. It has become one of the most important core values at Los Cenzontles to only teach a child a tradition with which they can fully participate; I understand how it feels to be treated as an outsider to my own heritage.

CHAPTER 6

●●●

PAPA'S DREAM, LOS LOBOS, AND LALO GUERRERO

A few months after our second trip to Veracruz in 1993, a record label contacted me to work on a children's album for Los Lobos. Although I had been involved with some studio recordings, I had little experience with the music industry at that time. The opportunity to work with the legendary group was both thrilling and terrifying.

I first learned about Los Lobos from college friends who exchanged bootleg cassettes of their albums. In a music industry that routinely ignores or segregates Mexican American artists, Los Lobos was breaking through not only with their unique rock sound but also their renditions of Mexican folk music, which they played with the same vitality and edge. Their 1987 version of "La Bamba" (plus other Ritchie Valens songs featured in Luis Valdez's hit movie about the singer's life) catapulted Los Lobos into the national consciousness, making an enormous impact not just in the Chicano community but well beyond. Many of our students began to play music because of that soundtrack.

For this new album, the label explained that, within the limits of the production budget, Los Lobos required that the songs be selected in advance, and this was to be my job. I had gotten good at researching folk music for Los Cenzontles, so I jumped into the project enthusiastically. The album required a storyline, so I mapped out a road trip from LA through Mexico and found music from the regions along the route that I thought children would enjoy. I recommended my brother Phillip to write the script, which became the colorful story of a grandfather taking his kids and grandkids to Mexico in a giant blimp, the Wooly Bully, to celebrate his eightieth birthday. Along the way they have adventures and sing songs in a variety of Mexican genres, including rancheras, cumbias, corridos, and sones from Tierra Caliente, Guerrero, and Veracruz, as well as a few rock songs.

On January 12, 1994, our son Emiliano was born, healthy and beautiful and surrounded by love. In many senses, he was a miracle child—bright, loving, and a joy to raise, and the only grandchild my parents would have. My mother, who came up from Glendale to help care for him, used to thank him for saving her from the Northridge earthquake, which had toppled her chimney during the time she was with us.

The earthquake also delayed the recording session with Los Lobos, which had already been held up for months by contract negotiations between the label and the artists. While on standby, the terms of my engagement were never discussed, but my responsibilities on the project kept growing. I was not raised to be overly concerned with contracts, and with few notable exceptions I normally do business without them, but in this case there were clear signs that I should have one. When I asked the label about it, I was scolded for being untrusting, which made me *feel* untrusting.

As the session date approached, I became increasingly uncomfortable not having a contract, so I gave the label my conditions and told them I would need the contract signed and faxed before I would come to Los Angeles. On the morning of the recording, it still had not arrived, so I skipped my flight and reminded them that I would come down only once the paperwork was complete. Moments later, the signed contract arrived by fax and I headed to the airport. When I landed in Southern California, the record label owner, who had been waiting for me, greeted me by asking, "Who the fuck do you think you are?" I replied, "I am the guy with the project and a contract," pointing to my briefcase of songs. "Do you want me to go back home?" He remained silent until lunch and then congratulated me for my business acumen. We headed to the home studio of Los Lobos member Cesar Rosas to record.

The public image of Los Lobos is of a group of tough guys from a tough neighborhood playing tough music. I entered the session feeling nervous not only because of that image (and my utter admiration for them) but also because of my lack of experience in the professional music world. I also did not understand the group's dynamics or how to relate to them. In a band that has played together for as long as Los Lobos, there is much that goes unspoken, and because there is no designated leader, finding consensus takes time, if it happens at all. For an outsider, especially one as green as I was, navigating their silent pauses was awkward, but they were patient with me and we began the process.

The album was recorded in steps, starting with basic rhythm tracks laid down while I provided a guide track to mark the sections. Then they overdubbed additional instruments and vocals. Members of the band came in and out of the studio as needed, otherwise waiting in different rooms of Cesar's spacious ranch-style home. David Hidalgo, who sang and played multiple instruments, including the violin and accordion, once excused himself to go to the store, saying that he would be right back . . . and didn't return until the next day. Little by little I began to learn how they worked, and I tried my best to adapt, and to trust that it would all get done. Lunch was always a favorite time for me because I got to know the group's members a little better, gathered around Cesar's kitchen table, often eating burritos from a local taqueria.

On the album, kids from Los Cenzontles sang the parts of the grandchildren. The budget to record them was limited, so I took them to a grungy studio in San Francisco's Mission District, not far from my apartment, that doubled as a rock nightclub, smelling of stale beer. Hugo Arroyo, a shy young teen at the time, had begun to take a more prominent role in the group because of his clear voice, easy nature, and natural approach to music, and I had him sing the child's solos on "El Pato" and "La Bamba." He was one of the kids who had begun taking guitar lessons because of the *La Bamba* movie and hit song, starting with me at the age of eight at Downer Elementary School. He was soft-spoken and intelligent, with a quick, impish sense of humor. In those days, most of my students did not stand out academically, but they were bright, and I provoked them with silly jokes and stories, watching to see if their reactions indicated they had a spark. Hugo had sparks in spades, though he lacked confidence when he was very young. In time, however, he built himself up through determination and hard work. I felt enormous pride that he would sing alongside David Hidalgo's brilliant, warm voice.

When considering who should play the role of the grandfather, Cesar suggested Lalo Guerrero, widely regarded as the godfather of Chicano music, and I was asked to invite him. When I called and introduced myself as Eugene Rodriguez, pronouncing my name in English, Lalo responded, "Do you mean, Rrrrodriguez?" emphasizing the rolled Spanish "R." I soon realized that he was just breaking my chops, and from there we developed a warm relationship as we worked together to create bilingual lyrics for many of the album's songs.

Lalo Guerrero, Mark Guerrero, Eugene Rodriguez, and Cesar Rosas recording vocals, 1994

Lalo, born on Christmas Eve in 1916, was an inspired casting choice for how much personality, musicality, warmth, and cultural history he added to the album. His career in many ways defines the Mexican American experience of the mid-twentieth century, beginning in 1939 with his first hit song, "Canción Mexicana," sung by Lucha Reyes. In the 1940s he wrote and recorded popular pachuco songs such as "Los Chucos Suaves" and "Marihuana Boogie," both of which later appeared in the iconic play and film *Zoot Suit*. In Mexico he was popular for his ardillitas, children's recordings in Spanish, which were similar to Alvin and the Chipmunks albums in the United States. And the parodies he wrote during the 1960s still resonate today for their political wit and charm. "No Chicanos on TV," set to the music based on Joyce Kilmer's poem "Trees," never fails to make me laugh.

In 1996, Los Lobos' *Papa's Dream*, a fun and authentic Chicano children's album, was nominated for a Grammy Award for Best Musical Album for Children, and it was an exciting time for Los Cenzontles. Our teens performed at a Grammy party at the nightclub Bimbo's in San Francisco, and Marie-Astrid and I attended the awards ceremony in Los Angeles (bringing one-year-old Emiliano with us to the reception at the Biltmore hotel). I remember sitting at the ceremony when they announced our category. I was next to Lalo, and he reached over and confided, "I want to win." I replied, "Me too." We did not win, but it was an honor to have made an album that introduced Los Lobos, Lalo Guerrero, Los Cenzontles, and our beautiful traditions to new generations of children.

Lalo continued to support us and perform with our youth group in the following years in the Bay Area and beyond. A native of Tucson, Arizona, he was longtime friends with Linda Ronstadt's father, Gilbert, and he had known Linda since she was a small child. On one of his visits to San Francisco, while staying at Linda's home, he called me to say, with a wisp of desperation, that there was nothing to drink there, and he asked if I could come get him to go have a beer.

We also continued to see Los Lobos over the years, and in 2008 they performed at Los Cenzontles to benefit our academy. I remember the moment when they began to play. I sat down on the side of the stage with a shot of tequila and wiped a tear from my eye, feeling that I had realized a long-held dream.

CHAPTER 7

●●●

JOY AND UNCERTAINTY IN
A CHANGING NEIGHBORHOOD

The first three months of 1994 were filled with a mix of emotions: great joy with the birth of our son Emiliano and the opportunity to record *Papa's Dream* with Los Lobos, and sadness following the murder of fifteen-year-old Cecilia Rios. But the year still had much more in store for us. Tensions were coming to a head with the host organization where our youth group was still based. I considered my accomplishments with Los Cenzontles a contribution to the organization, but its director seemed to see them as a threat, casting me in a suspicious light. For example, I was told that our trips to Mexico were unfair to the African American students, because they could not go to Africa. Of course, we would have been happy to support them if they set out to make it happen, but that did not seem to be the point. In multicultural settings, I have long witnessed people of color being pitted against each other and confronted with contorted rules and twisted ethical arguments to keep us in line. I felt as if a tightening web was being spun around me.

At a meeting in March 1994 I was given an ultimatum: to either submit in writing to accepting further restrictions with the *Papa's Dream* recording or be fired. I refused. I was provided a final opportunity to meet with one of the director's advisors, who simply told me to do as I was instructed. I responded that their demands were arbitrary and I would not sign. The advisor began to raise his voice, saying, "Who the hell do you think you are? [The director] gave you everything. You are nothing outside this center!" I was prepared to lose my job over the matter, but not to be humiliated or abused. When I verbally defended myself, he grew increasingly agitated until at last he stood up, grabbed onto my sweater, and tried to stab me with a sharpened pencil he had taken from the table, while others in attendance, including Gilberto Gutiérrez, held him back. The advisor started yelling, "I'll show you how we treat you. You're just a Chicano. You're not even a real Mexican." After that meeting, I was fired and a "real" Mexican was brought in to replace me.

Reading my contemporaneous notes on that meeting while preparing to write this book revives the feeling that I had lived with throughout those years, and beyond—being made to feel like an intruder in a world within which I fully belonged. The multicultural model promises inclusion and equality, but, in reality, it often reinforces segregation and stereotypes by defining groups by our superficial differences, akin to the "It's a Small World" ride at Disneyland. And underlying this model rooted in European colonialism, we minority cultures are "curated" within a hierarchy of authenticity, controlled by the values of the majority culture. This widespread system is then protected and enforced by people of many races and ethnicities who find privilege within it.

Given these restraints, there was little room for my vision of using our traditions as a means of self- and community realization and expression. The advisor had articulated what I had long understood: that within this system I would always be lesser, regardless of my accomplishments, because I was not born in Mexico; I could never be "authentic." But most painful to me was that many within the arts field overlooked the injustices that I was enduring because they were committed under the banner of multiculturalism, the goals of which they felt were more important than even the ethical treatment of the people that multiculturalism claimed to benefit.

The threat did not feel idle. I knew I was taking a risk in standing up for myself, especially as there are severe career consequences for Latinos who do not comply, but the consequences for not standing up are often worse. Internalizing humiliation builds resentment that not only corrodes us as individuals but also damages our relationships—too heavy a price to pay. I only wish I had learned to not let it cause me pain. The shame, after all, is not ours. In a sense, I was fortunate that this crisis provided me with a clear choice: I would either give up Los Cenzontles or become independent and expand our work.

In June 1994, guided by a how-to book published by NOLO Press, I incorporated Los Cenzontles Mexican Arts Center as a 501(c)(3) nonprofit organization. All of my students and colleagues came with me, including Gilberto Gutiérrez, who renounced a grant from the National Endowment for the Arts, and Alicia Marines, who left her job as a program coordinator to become our administrative director. Born and raised in Richmond, she had deep connections to the community and would remain committed to Los Cenzontles while her children were part of the program. I learned to be an executive director on the job, with no income the first year and hardly more the second. To earn a living during this time, I taught guitar at California State Prison Solano and occasionally performed with community groups.

To house our fledgling program, we rented space by the hour at Maple Hall, a Spanish colonial–style facility that also served as City Hall for neighboring San Pablo. We shared the space with senior citizens, San Pablo's largest demographic at that time, who held midday bingo games there. In the afternoon, we brought in our instruments and art supplies, held classes, and then carried everything out immediately afterward. We also expanded our class offerings, adding folk arts, and opened up enrollment to younger children. A few months later, in September, we hosted our first community event in Maple Hall's beautiful adjacent garden. Instead of commemorating Mexican Independence Day, we celebrated our own "Cultural Independence Day."

Los Cenzontles, San Pablo Civic Center, 1995. Photo by David Do

The mid-1990s was a time of great change in our neighborhood, and in many parts of the country, because of the historic immigration from Mexico that came after the passage of

NAFTA. I remember the debates around whether or not to ratify the treaty. Some said it would provide opportunity for both the US and Mexico and that it would lower the price of goods for the poor here. Others said it would intensify exploitation and radically change the Mexican economy. In retrospect, it appears to have done both.

●●●

Our community was more than ready for its own cultural center, and there was a palpable sense of enthusiasm when we opened, especially among the teens who roamed the neighborhood looking for something to do while their immigrant parents were busy working and trying to figure out their new lives. Alicia could often be seen driving a station wagon full of kids to and from Maple Hall. Hector Espinoza, who had been my guitar student at Lincoln Elementary School, appeared at our classes, now a gangly teen wearing Dickies pants, Ben Davis work shirts or button-downs buttoned to the top, a belt with its strap hanging down (the longer the better), and a hairnet. Hugo Arroyo, whose confidence had been bolstered by his flourishing mastery of the jarana, now began learning a host of other instruments, including the guitarrón and the sousaphone. Lucina Rodriguez and Fabiola Trujillo, who would become core members of our organization, both joined us as fifteen-year-old students, in 1994 and 1995, respectively.

During previous waves of immigration, many Mexican immigrants found ways to hide their presence from the larger society. But this new group wore their Mexicanidad loudly and proudly, perhaps because their sheer numbers created a critical mass. Teens wore cowboy hats and boots and danced rancheras, zapateados, and quebradita, which was characterized at that time as the "dirty dancing" of banda music. The newcomers celebrated anniversaries, weddings, baptisms, and quinceañeras with live music at their homes and at rental halls. I was fascinated to get to know how they lived, suspecting that they might provide me insight into the world my grandparents were part of when they had arrived in the United States seven decades before.

To accommodate the musical tastes of our evolving student base, we also added classes in more genres of Mexican music. In our first year, Gilberto Gutiérrez taught son jarocho, and Silvia González de León taught art. Each week, the first family of Bay Area mariachi, Francisco "Pato" Díaz and his children Juan and Carla, drove from San Jose to share their deep knowledge of mariachi music with our students. Pato was a patient, gifted teacher whom the kids liked and respected, and his group Mariachi Azteca de San Jose would continue to support our events in the years to come. If it were my choice, Pato and his family would be awarded the National Heritage Fellowship for his decades of service to the community.

We also began teaching the popular music and dance of the bandas de viento (wind bands, known more commonly as just "bandas"), which were popular with immigrant kids. Bandas include three trumpets, three valve trombones, three clarinets, a sousaphone, and two percussionists, on tarolas and tambora. There were not many musicians in our area who taught traditional banda, so we recruited local musicians Tom Fuglestad, Mara Fox, and Juan Ceballos—who did not know the banda style—and they taught the teens instrument technique while remaining open to the styles the kids were listening to.

Some in the community criticized us for teaching banda music, calling it música corriente (low-class music). Of course, the origins of most folk music are from the "lower" classes, so I didn't see a problem. I was thrilled that the kids were excited to learn. It was what they listened and danced to; instead of garage rock bands, they formed garage bandas, and Los Cenzontles was the place to learn techniques that supported their interests.

We were not trying to change them or "elevate" their musical tastes, just support them.

The influx of immigrants exposed and exacerbated many class and cultural divides that already existed in the community. Latino leaders to whom we appealed for support were calling for pan-Latin identity, while immigrants tended to identify more locally, boasting the names of their pueblos of origin on their vehicle bumper stickers. Acculturated Latinos were drawn to the more sophisticated urban sounds of Latin jazz and salsa, and some seemed embarrassed by the regional Mexican music enjoyed by the newcomers. Most immigrants steered clear of the political organizing pushed by US-born Latinos, and as hard as I tried to convince Latino leaders that this cultural wave was a historic opportunity for investment and partnership, the new-comers were largely viewed with a degree of condescension.

One evening in December 1994, we produced our first Las Posadas, a traditional reenactment of the Nativity in which one group of musicians and singers portrays the parts of Mary and Joseph seeking refuge, while another group portrays the inn-keepers who refuse them entry. Our students, teachers, and community members moved from arch to arch that lined the San Pablo Civic Center plaza requesting/denying refuge. At the final stop, the migrants were finally welcomed inside Maple Hall, which had been decorated by our art students, who had also made candy-stuffed piñatas that would later be gleefully broken by joyful children. At the party, our students and teach-ers performed mariachi, son jarocho, and banda music and dance. For our Mexican American students, it was a taste of Mexico, where many had never been. For the Mexicans, it was like being back home.

While writing about 1994, it is difficult for me to tease out the many life-changing events, intertwined so closely in time, that suddenly launched me into another orbit of purpose and responsibility. Marie-Astrid and I now had a child to care for, and we had hope for the future. Once Emiliano began to walk, we moved our family from San Francisco to a rented house in Richmond with room for him to grow and explore. Our black chihuahua, Polka Dot, whom we got at a flea market while raising money for our trip to Pajapan, also joined us during that year, as did our cat, Poochie Pie.

Marie-Astrid, Eugene, and Emiliano Rodriguez, 1996. Photo by Roland Sarlot

Los Cenzontles continued to strengthen and grow at Maple Hall. We added classes and new students, and we hosted regular cultural events in the garden plaza of San Pablo Civic Center, attracting a diverse cross section of our neighborhood. Every step that we took would be alongside many others as our work, and network, grew. Los Cenzontles was now an independent nonprofit organization. No longer having a singular obstacle against which to struggle, I began to learn more about the dimensions of leadership as I took on the challenge of finding resources to support our program and of navigating community politics. Alicia tried to accommodate the various interests that

were attracted to our rapid growth, including advocates, politicians, and stage parents, but I was not interested in making
compromises that detracted from our focus. It was clear to me
that what was happening with the kids was extraordinary and
unique, and deserving of our exclusive support and protection.
Los Cenzontles was gaining strength, but it was still very fragile. And although our budget grew slowly, we were making an
outsized impact and being recognized beyond our community,
something that was boosted by the 1995 release of our album *Con
Su Permiso, Señores*, on renowned folk label Arhoolie Records.
Its founder, Chris Strachwitz, became a prominent advocate for
our work as we became part of his community and he became
part of ours.

In 1997, with binational funding, we produced the Festival of
Youth in the Tradition, which presented workshops and performances by youth groups from around California and Veracruz,
as well as by major musicians from the mariachi, son jarocho,
and banda traditions. Featured guests included Lalo Guerrero,
Graciela Beltrán, Yolanda del Río, Grupo Mono Blanco,
Conjunto Hueyapan, Mariachi Azteca de San Jose, Banda Rio
Verde, and Los Cenzontles. The shows were held at various local
venues, the largest of which was the huge Richmond Memorial
Auditorium, with full professional sound and lights. That concert was another step in expanding our footprint, and for our
kids it was the most thrilling leap of all—right onto the biggest
stage in their own neighborhood, in front of their friends and
families, just as they were coming into their own.

CHAPTER 8

●❤●

SPACE

Los Cenzontles did not have its own facility until 1998, nine years after it began, so I have considered the concept of space from many points of view. Space exists within our minds as we conceive ideas, and between individuals when we share them. Space is the canvas for the movement of dance, and it is where sound vibrates within an acoustic instrument or human body. The tarima, which people dance on and musicians gather around, proves that transformative space can be portable. Our facility would become a place where children could find space within themselves to grow.

After four years of renting by the hour, our presence at Maple Hall was becoming untenable, especially as the organization continued to grow. Although our children and teens coexisted with the senior citizens without serious incident, we needed a permanent place to store our expanding inventory of instruments and supplies, and to further strengthen our work and identity. San Pablo's city manager, Rory Robinson, identified a local landlord, Al Dias, who would lease us a 3,700-square-foot storefront in the nearby Dias Plaza strip mall at a discounted rent, half of which the city would pay for our first few years. Al was a gregarious, old-school leader in the Portuguese community that had dominated San Pablo politics for years. Formerly a city council member and county supervisor, Al presented us with a half-page handwritten lease, and he regularly visited us, telling familiar jokes with a handshake and a smile. San Pablo's transition to a majority Latino population made for many interesting dynamics during those years, but Al Dias knew which way the winds were blowing. His generosity made a lasting impact on us, and even after his passing in 2003, his widow, June, and son, George, made sure to extend our favorable lease conditions to remain in effect even after the family sold the property.

We transformed the storefront, which was formerly a liquor store and was wedged between a Round Table Pizza franchise, a laundromat, and a vacant space that had once been a discount grocery store. Our total renovation budget of $25,000—for supplies and equipment—was contributed by Leandro Duran, a local Chicano attorney who had recently won a major legal settlement. Alicia and I recruited a large volunteer workforce from students and their friends and family members. Hugo Arroyo, Jorge Navarrete, Sergio Garcia, Melvin Cuevas, Ruben Rangel, and sisters Violeta, Monica, and Gabriela, with their father, Cruz Contreras, demolished walls, dismantled an industrial freezer unit that once cooled beer, wine, meats, and dairy products, and ripped out a worn carpet that showed evidence a dog had once lived there. Eight-year-old Blanca Hernandez's parents, Fernando Hernandez and Luz Morales, helped us salvage discarded light fixtures and furniture from San Francisco's Univision building, which was being relocated, and young

Benito Marines and his crew of electricians who were learning
the trade wired the building. My uncle Roland traveled from
Southern California to manage the project, and he brought
volunteers Tom Montello, who oversaw electrical, and Adrian
Lewis, who mounted drywall, plus a company to install a new
HVAC system.

New signage at Los Cenzontles, San Pablo

Comanaging the project was Andy Kridle, a mechanical
engineer who had been my guitar student in the mid-1980s, and
whose hands I have never seen clean of oil and other work parti-
cles. When Emiliano was little, he referred to Andy as half man
and half nature, an impression Andy gave through his affable
character, full beard, and insatiable curiosity. Andy's partner,
Barbara Selhorst, whose previous job was managing a trucking
company, would eventually become our business manager.

Dan Aldrich, a friend of my cousin Roland, drove from
Washington state to install the hardwood floor made of white
oak, assisted by my brothers-in-law Christoph Do and Tony
Ternullo, all of whom volunteered their time. To me, this
expansive floor connects us to each other, like the enormous

underground mushrooms that connect forests in the Pacific Northwest. Dan worked for three days straight and drove back home after his final shift. He would later die in an explosion at a fuel refinery in Anacortes, Washington. Five years before that, Tony also died tragically, in an automobile accident. Our facility is inhabited by the spirits of many people who generously contributed to its creation, and we honor them through our dedication to our work.

●●●

A visitor entering our academy will first be struck by its welcoming feel and visual beauty, due in large part to Marie-Astrid's ingenious floor tile pattern for the reception area and the distinctive color design for the walls, which she painted herself with assistance from our singers Lucina Rodriguez, Fabiola Trujillo, Violeta Contreras, and Kristal Gray. I insisted that we model our floor plan after a Mexican plaza, centered around a common space that features our hardwood floor—used for zapateado dance—and surrounded by classrooms. Adjoining the floor is a stage, raised three feet, with plenty of room for musicians and dancers.

Having our own facility made it possible for us to stabilize and blossom. We could host events whenever we wished, and we could record ourselves in our makeshift recording studio. In 1998 alone we released three albums: *Volando en los Cafetales*, a collection of sones jarochos; *Hypnotizada*, a collection of popular and original songs performed by our banda; and *Amor, Paz, y Sinceridad*, a collection of a capella alabanzas—folk songs of praise, rooted in medieval times—that our young women singers learned from folk artist Gisela Farías Luna during her three-month residency. The cover art of *Amor, Paz, y Sinceridad*, which features a beautiful pastel of the Virgen de Guadalupe, was made by David Flury, an artist I had met while teaching guitar at a California state prison. David nurtured his skills while in the Arts in Corrections program, and since his release, he has dedicated himself to art and giving back to the community. He agreed to create cover art for this book in appreciation for my kindness during a dark period in his life.

Marie-Astrid says that creating art is like finding extra rooms within yourself, and I hope that our students can do the same within our program. Her artistic approach to the folk arts, which is deeply personal, artistically demanding, quietly intense, organic, and healing, has shaped our work on many levels. Her teaching style is both individualized to the student and cognizant of the importance of a cooperative culture in the classroom. She is infinitely patient with her students but will not abide capricious behavior that distracts others, as each student deserves to have the space to cultivate their skills and imaginations.

Her jewelry classes are a reflective time for children to develop refined skills and creativity, and her approach is steeped in the philosophies of early childhood education that she studied as a young adult. Her upbringing within the Vietnamese community in the suburbs of Paris taught her the values of working within a cultural community, and her healing approach to art is directly related to her personal experience with trauma. Her multiracial identity continues to inform her sensitivities about inclusion and belonging, and about the nuanced and dynamic role that culture plays in our lives.

There is nothing I can write about her vision that she could not write many times better. The parents and children who invest time in Marie-Astrid's art classes develop a deep respect for textiles and folk arts. Some of our students tell us they have learned to connect with their Mexican grandmothers through their shared love of sewing or knitting. Others say they have learned to value the work and skill of the people who make the Mexican blouses they buy in stores. Ultimately, the lessons that Marie-Astrid teaches are essential: to weave ourselves into the fabric of life using our hands and eyes, and to find place and meaning through relying on and strengthening our resourcefulness.

In this way, Los Cenzontles' facility mirrors the work that we do with children. From the outside, it appears ordinary, but from the inside you can see that it has been made extraordinary because of the care that people have invested into it. Archival photos and album covers hanging on our walls tell our history and legacy, and our classrooms are lined with works of art, art supplies, and instruments that we use to do our work. When I see community organizations with unkempt or sterile facilities, I question the value that they have for their work and their community.

We teach our students to be hosts and stewards of our space because it cultivates a sense of belonging. Our teachers have them pull out and put away folding chairs before and after each class, and parents tidy up our theater after recitals without prompting. After one event, I remember seeing two-year-old Clarissa Ortega pushing chairs to her father, Juan, who was hanging them in their racks, an act of collaborative culture in which children learn by watching and participating. In fact, it was a parent-led fundraiser that had purchased the chairs and rack in the first place. Entrusting our children with the responsibility of stewardship is especially important given that many in our community are not welcomed in certain public spaces. I believe that seeing everyone as guardians of our society and world—rather than treating some as outsiders or guests—is fundamental to democracy and equality.

From 2014 to 2017, Los Cenzontles launched a capital campaign to renovate and expand our facility, this time with more philanthropic support. We purchased the lease of the adjacent laundromat, adding 1,300 square feet, which we used to create an office, a lovely kitchen adorned with colorful Mexican tiles, and an art room. Marie-Astrid redesigned the color scheme and floor tiling, we reinforced the soundproofing between the classrooms, and we upgraded the HVAC system. Helen and John Meyer, of the internationally renowned Meyer Sound, donated a magnificent sound system for our theater, which we use for performances and film screenings.

For part of this renovation (again managed by Andy Kridle), Gregorio "Goyo" Reyes, the father of longtime students Isabel and Selena, led the construction team. Goyo had arrived in Richmond from Mexico in the late 1990s, and as a teenager without family support, he often found himself staying at the homes of his high school classmates, some of whom were in our banda program. He tells me that he always wanted to take classes at Los Cenzontles but was busy working and learning English. After high school, he became a general contractor, and in appreciation for our work with his daughters, he oversaw our renovation pro bono.

Some organizations rely on expensive architectural design to convey the value of their work. We do so with the art that we create and the manner in which we take care of it. And, like most homes in our community, the facility is fragile. The back cinderblock wall lets in moisture, making those rooms cold and damp, and the roof regularly leaks in the rain, putting our equipment and instruments at risk. But we are resourceful and grateful. Los Cenzontles is a special place not because it gives off an appearance of power or wealth but because it embodies the spirit of community cooperation—a resource that is transitory but also, if nurtured with care, timeless.

CHAPTER 9

●●●

PASAJERO, A JOURNEY
OF TIME AND MEMORY

Since the mid-1990s, in the wake of the mass migration that resulted from NAFTA, many Mexicans—and the traditions they carried—traveled far past their regions of origin, both within and outside of Mexico. The difficulty of crossing the US–Mexico border reinforced a sense of Mexican identity for those living in the US, while evolving digital technology, which made long-distance communication more affordable, allowed many living in Mexico to increasingly adopt American sensibilities. It may not be too surprising, then, that it was Mexican Americans who spearheaded revivals of Mexico's cultural traditions.

Following our success in planting seeds of the fandango jarocho in California, I set out to find, and work with, master artists from other regions of Mexico who had deep family roots to their ancestral cultures. Because many people in San

Pablo and Richmond were from the state of Jalisco, I especially wanted to find someone to teach us an older style of mariachi, though I didn't really believe I would find anyone, or even if such a person still existed. Historically, mariachi had started as a local, rural string quartet from the ranches of Jalisco, but in the 1930s and 1940s, it transitioned into an urban orchestra. By the time I was looking for mariachi teachers for our students, I figured that any remnants of the genre's humble origins had become extinct. And if any such maestros were still alive, it would be highly unlikely that they lived in the Bay Area . . . and yet that is exactly what we found in Julián González Saldaña. When local mariachi chronicler Jonathan Clark told me about an elder, recently arrived from Mexico, who was eager to share his knowledge of an old mariachi style, I was both thrilled and skeptical.

The core members of Los Cenzontles first visited don Julián in his small apartment on the San Francisco peninsula in the year 2000. He presented us with a small piece of paper with a handwritten list of sones abajeños (lowland sones) that he could teach us, and then he told us his personal history, showing us photos, awards, and a recording he had made in Jalisco with a group of elders called Los Centenarios. He had learned the original mariachi style—a string ensemble with no trumpets—within his family on a hacienda on the ranch of Camichines, Municipality of Tecolotlán, one of the original cradles of the mariachi tradition. And he had lived much of his life as a jinete, or cowboy.

We returned to his apartment weekly to learn his instrumental, vocal, and dance stylings, which were more akin to what you'd expect for an improvised, old-timey string band, rather than the contemporary mariachi orchestras, which rely on fixed musical arrangements. Gathered in don Julian's modest living room, Tregar Otton learned the first violin parts, Hugo

Julián González Saldaña

Arroyo learned the guitarrón bass and first voice parts, and I played the five-string strummed vihuela. Lucina Rodriguez learned the dance steps and movements in his tiny kitchenette, the only space that was not carpeted. Don Julián played second violin, sang vocals, and guided us from memory. Whereas mariachi vocals are now commonly associated with the broad vibrato of European opera that was introduced by popular singers in Mexican film in the 1930s and '40s, the original vocals were sung in a more natural style. Don Julián taught Hugo, Lucina, and Fabiola Trujillo the vocal phrasing and straight tone with which to sing the sones and rancheras characteristic of Mexico's ranches. Within a few years, we would not only tour the US sharing what we had learned but also reintroduce the tradition back to Jalisco, where it had been largely forgotten.

Renowned mariachi Natividad Cano twice traveled from Southern California to learn about our work with don Julián. He wondered out loud how Julián, who was younger than he, could know more about the old tradition. The answer was that Nati was from Guadalajara, while Julián was from a ranch, where traditions were more protected from the changes of modernity.

In his mid-sixties when we met him, Julián was of medium stature, with a thin mustache, and strong as an ox. Always helpful and full of cheer, he insisted on carrying our hardwood tarima to performances by himself. Once, a group of Berkeley women scolded us for making an old man lift such a heavy object. They did not know that don Julián would be offended at even the suggestion that he needed help. Once, after he had moved to a tough neighborhood in Richmond to be closer to Los Cenzontles, don Julián was knocked down and robbed by a teenager. Julián got up, chased the boy many blocks to his house, and called the police, who did nothing about it, much to Julián's surprise.

His teaching approach was not formal, nor was it always clear (he had never taught before), but he was passionate about presenting us with accurate information. He showed us what he remembered, and often corrected himself the following week. We all had previously learned to play contemporary mariachi music, but this was something different. Most of the sones did not, for instance, place the bass notes on downbeats, as in modern mariachi, giving the groove a unique feel. Julián also taught Lucina how the steps and movements were danced socially on the ranch, which bore little resemblance to the choreographed ballet folklórico style that was adapted for the stage. He did not read music but was tickled to see Tregar write out the violin parts; Julián referred to the notation as "bolitas," or little balls, marveling at the system's efficiency. During rehearsals without written music, we could not jump to a specific measure to work out a given section, as would a classical ensemble, so Julián always had us start over from the beginning. Learning by rote takes a lot of time, but it builds solid brain and muscle memory, and so it was no wonder that he could still remember violin bowings after forty years.

There are many nuances distinguishing the various musical styles of Mexico's regions, and these differences deserve respectful attention; if you teach diverse cultural music with standard pedagogy, everything will sound the same. There are pauses, rhythmic skips, lilts, and accents that provide insights about the musical cultures and lifestyles that nurtured them. Even within the same region, families and towns have their own variances, as do individual musicians and dancers. There is a common misperception that folk music follows strict orthodoxy. But in my experience, deep roots musicians place a premium on individual expression within a communal identity. Don Julián also described how instrumental and dance gestures mimicked movements of the animals he had worked with as a jinete. These are important distinctions to make available to our children, who will never experience the lives of our ancestors. When teaching Lucina to dance the original mariachi son abajeño, he demonstrated and explained, for example, that campesinos did not dance with the erect posture of the European ballet, as do folklórico dancers, but are instead bent in reverence, characteristic of humble Mexicans.

There was a moment when don Julián was teaching us the venerable son "El Pasajero" when I grew suspicious of his knowledge. He insisted on dropping a beat between the instrumental and vocal sections, something that made little musical sense when looked at from a standardized point of view. So I searched for an old recording of the son and found a version by Mariachi Tapatío de José Marmolejo from 1939. To my surprise and delight, there it was: the dropped beat. Julián was vindicated.

In the 1930s, Mexico's ruling party enlisted the mariachi, from among many regional musical styles, to become the official symbol of the country and its dominant political party. To assume that lofty role, its sound and image was gentrified. The musicians, who were peasants from the countryside, were required, by force of law, to wear the charro outfit of upper-class horsemen when performing within the limits of Mexico City. The charros protested that their fine regalia had been appropriated by peasants, whose typical garb was simple clothing made of manta (coarse cotton cloth), plus straw hats and huaraches. But Mexico's rulers sought to portray an idealized peasantry, just as the Ballet Folklórico de México, modeled after the Soviet Ballet, codified the diversity of Mexico's local clothing into official costumes organized by states, which are politically, not culturally, drawn.

Modern mariachi borrows much of its violin technique from classical music, and its complex arrangements and harmonies from contemporary popular music. The sones, which people used to dance to at length on the ranches, were shortened and often arranged into medleys to demonstrate versatility and virtuosity. The repertory increasingly became international, and less regional, to show Mexico's sophistication. In my mind, the current movement of mariachi education in schools is more an ethnic variation of orchestral music rather than actual folk music. This is not necessarily a problem, but if we play all music with a standardized approach, the individual musical styles lose their distinct identities. As veteran mariachi Benjamin Torres was quoted in our film *Pasajero*, "Nowadays they are good readers, good musicians, and all that. But they've taken away the flavor of the old mariachi that is mariachi."

The function of traditional music and dance also changes when it transitions toward pageantry. Playing and dancing music, according to Julián, was the rare opportunity for campesinos to experience moments of joy in an otherwise miserable existence. Mexico's poor have been humiliated and exploited for centuries, and on the hacienda where don Julián lived, he explained, the rich could abuse and kill the poor with impunity. Children like himself were forbidden, by law, to be educated past the fourth grade, and most of the people spent their days working. For these beleaguered people, music and dance were essential to maintaining their humanity. It is important to understand these original functions of our traditions so we do not erase the resilient strength embedded within them, nor make them inaccessible to communities that still need them.

As we had learned studying the rural son jarocho, the music and dance stylings of Mexican campesinos, though stigmatized as low-class, are of no less quality than their gentrified derivatives. When the mariachi transitioned from a rural quartet to an urban orchestra, Mexican people continued to embrace it as indelible to community life in Mexico *and* in the Mexican diaspora. For me, this adaptation demonstrates community ingenuity, which is to be celebrated. But I also believe we must learn to recognize the power and beauty of our original, unadorned rural folk traditions and accept that they were born of the working poor. The value of our culture is not embedded in the golden thread of regalia borrowed from the upper classes, European affectations, or lofty political rhetoric. Rather, it comes from the humility, creativity, and perseverance of hardworking people who managed to make remarkable music and art in the face of the abuse and humiliation heaped upon them for centuries. It is this resilience that is the true gift and power of our intangible heritage.

Los Cenzontles Mariachi Tradicional, circa 2002. Photo by Armando Quintero

●◗●

In April of 2003, our Los Cenzontles traditional mariachi traveled to Jalisco to return this old style back to its homeland, an ambitious proposal whose risks frightened some of the younger members of our group. How would we, a group of Mexican Americans, be received? Despite this uncertainty, I felt that we were ready to at least try, and if we were successful, I was sure the trip would be historic and impactful. We contracted Mexican filmmaker Ricardo Braojos, recommended by my brother Phillip, to document our adventure.

To plan the tour, we hired a guide in Jalisco who had once been a government official with the state ministry of culture. He organized a tour of nine cities and pueblos in Jalisco and Nayarit, and he knew many of the veteran musicians we hoped to interview. Our telephone conversations gave me no reason to suspect any problems. He had built a career promoting traditional music and musicians from the region, and was himself an amateur musician trying to revive the old traditions. When he heard us playing live in the hotel the night before the tour began, he was overwhelmed by the quality and authenticity of our playing. Soon, however, as he became increasingly drunk, his praise for our music got louder, laced with aggression, and revealing of a dark envy. He seemed unable to reconcile his admiration for our work with the fact that most of us were Mexican Americans.

On the first day of the tour, the guide arrived at our bus hours late, already intoxicated. He soon began menacing our group, which included my son Emiliano, now nine years old. He also made sexual innuendos to our female members. During our first performance in the plaza of Tamazulita, a small, humble pueblo, he humiliated the guest musicians onstage whom we had hired to open the show, publicly scolding them for not being as good or as traditional as Los Cenzontles. He also made vulgar comments about our violinist Tregar Otton's last name, saying that it sounded like "joto," a disparaging term for gay men.

At the aftershow dinner in a local home, I took him aside and explained that his behavior was unacceptable and had to change. He then became even more abusive, stood up, put his face against mine, and threw his shot glass of tequila on the floor, shattering it. Marie-Astrid and Fabiola both rose to settle him down as I noticed that a policeman, seated in the room with a long gun, was observing the scene. I grew very nervous, as I knew the severe consequences that I, a foreigner, would suffer if I were to run afoul of the law. I was relieved when the policeman nodded to me, signaling his support for us.

Once outside the home, I notified our guide that we would continue the tour without him. His response, a mix of drunken rage and sobbing self-pity, frightened us all. He blamed his behavior on his twenty-six-year-old mistress, who had recently left him. When I did not respond with sympathy, he accused me of being cold and called me "gringo prieto" (black gringo) as we got on the bus and left him behind. That night, we hardly slept in our hotel for fear that he might retaliate in a country that was not ours. Shaken and feeling vulnerable for the safety of our group, I considered canceling the tour and going home. The next morning, I called my father for support and expressed my gratitude to my grandparents for leaving a country that would allow such an abusive man to rise to a position of respect and authority in state government. In fact, such people are a common feature in Mexico's layered system of control. Through local bosses called caciques, this hierarchy continues to haunt the country, and the mindsets of Mexicans everywhere.

The next day, we got back on the bus without the guide but also without an itinerary, leaving our tour plans in the dark. I never considered reinviting the man back on the bus, although our hired crew had tried to do so behind my back, in consultation with Tregar, the only Anglo in our group, whom the crew, and many others, had assumed was our director. I then remembered that I had the telephone number of the guide's estranged wife, who lived in Mexico City. I called and asked her if she would fax us a copy of the itinerary. She did so, fully understanding our situation and sympathizing with us. We successfully continued our journey free from negativity.

The rest of the tour was arduous but immensely satisfying as we crisscrossed the arid region through fields of agave, sugar, and corn. Although this ancient land, checkered with ominous volcanos and historic pueblos, looked exotic to me, we found people in nearly every town, no matter how remote, who had relatives who had recently moved to the US. We were all much more connected than I had imagined.

We began our days traveling in the relative cool of the morning and arrived at our destinations in the blazing midafternoon heat. Our crew set up our sound system and lights in the outdoor spaces provided to us. Sometimes they erected temporary stages, and other times we performed in front of the town kiosk in the main plaza. Our musicians checked the sound while Marie-Astrid prepared our costumes, created by her and her mother, France, based on Julián's descriptions of what mariachis used to wear. Then, close to showtime, while the opening band played, we dressed, tuned up, and readied ourselves for the performance. Our shows were always well attended, and our six musicians and four dancers were sharp, nimble, and graceful. Hugo and Julián sang sones, rancheras, and corridos in duet, as did Fabiola and Lucina. Lucina and her brother Cristian Rodriguez danced in the traditional style with buoyant energy and grace. Our teenaged student Andrea Luna and a guest male dancer, Salvador Contreras, whom Lucina had trained before the tour, danced admirably as well.

When we were not performing, we took time to meet with and interview elders who could tell us about the old days of the mariachi. One, who refused to be interviewed on camera, told us that when "foreign" harmonies were introduced into the repertory, replacing Jalisco's native music, a generation of musicians retired. We also met Trinidad Ríos Aguayo, a mariachi in his late nineties, from Tepic, Nayarit. His body was frail and his eyes cloudy, but his wit remained sharp. When I asked him to describe what mariachi musicians were like in his youth, he replied, "Well, they weren't fat like you. They were workers." He was right, of course. In the countryside, there was no professional class of musicians. Laborers made the music.

Each town that we visited selected a family to host our meals. In the pueblo of Concepción de Buenos Aires, in Los Altos de Jalisco, we met Teresa Maldonado, an older woman who prepared us breakfast. After we men left doña Teresa's home, she began to sing in a beautifully unaffected manner in front of the women of Los Cenzontles who remained in her kitchen. Marie-Astrid immediately understood that this was a moment we were looking for. She sent for the crew, who returned to film Teresa singing "Cautiva y Triste" (Captive and Sad) at her kitchen table while wearing an apron. She spoke about her lifelong love of music and said that, as a child, she'd had to silence her voice in the presence of her father for fear of punishment. For me, the scene captures the essence of music's enduring and intimate power, which in this case was revealed only because she had been among women.

The tour was also challenged by a health condition of our dancer Cristian, who suffered a series of epileptic seizures both on- and offstage. One major episode landed him in the hospital, forcing him to miss our performance in don Julián's adopted pueblo of Tecolotlán (Land of the Owls), something Cristian regrets to this day. In Guadalajara, we were performing outdoors in the Plaza de Armas, with many of Cristian and Lucina's

Mexican family members in attendance, when Cristian began to stiffen up in seizure while dancing. Lucina discretely waved to her family members, who escorted him off of the tarima to wait until it passed, and the rest of the audience hardly noticed. It never occurred to me to exclude him from our group because of his health issues; we were there to take care of each other.

The public's reaction to our performances was charged with emotion. Elders were tearfully moved to experience music and dance they had not heard or seen for decades. Young people, unaware of their own traditions, were inspired to see them performed by other young people. Many congratulated us for reviving a tradition so far from its home. Julián arrived at his adopted pueblo of Tecolotlán like a returning hero. As he said on our bus for the film cameras, "After my wife died, I decided to go to California and take a chance. I left home alone, and now I return in good company."

Before a series of strokes forced Julián to retire to his pueblo, we had recorded five albums of traditional mariachi with him, performed his repertory nationally and in Mexico, and created the documentary film *Pasajero, A Journey of Time and Memory*, which recounted our trip to Jalisco. The film did not include the harrowing backstory with our tour guide, an incident that had so vividly demonstrated the humiliation that traditional musicians are often forced to endure in Mexico while pursuing support for their work. But these difficulties only reinforced my resolve to promote tradition as a means of independence and dignity and to protect our work from the forces of paternalism and control. Not all traditions or customs are good. We must strive to nurture the best of them, and the best in ourselves.

The 2004 release of our film *Pasajero, A Journey of Time and Memory* was met with enthusiasm and surprise. It is a film that portrays our folk culture and community members with rare authenticity—groundbreaking at a time when most Latino advocacy films portrayed us as either idealized victims or sanitized heroes. Immediately after a screening at an international arts conference in Oaxaca City sponsored by the Rockefeller Foundation, the audience sat quietly, left speechless by (some told us) the beauty and power of the film's honesty.

Because we had no access to broadcast distribution, I sent messages to a number of PBS affiliates via the Contact Us buttons on their websites. Station manager Jerry Lee at KVPT Fresno responded and agreed to broadcast our film during a pledge drive, at which I appeared as a guest. I still remember how the Latina host cautiously prepared viewers beforehand, describing the film as portraying "rustic culture." Immediately after it aired, we learned that it had attracted a record number of new Latino subscribers to the station, a boost that led to the film's distribution to PBS affiliates around the country.

Because of the outsized role that mariachi music has come to play commercially and politically, it is often laden with the trappings of power and status. But within that massive shadow sits our work with Julián González and the lesson that even within just one humble man can exist a cultural legacy worthy of our respect and attention. About our work with don Julián, mariachi chronicler Jonathan Clark cited Acts 4:11: "The stone the builders rejected has become the cornerstone of the new temple."

On the afternoon of October 12, 2022, don Julián's son Faustino called to say that his father's health had deteriorated and that he wanted to speak with us before he entered the ambulance that would take him to the hospital. We called Julián on his daughter's cellphone and told him that we loved and appreciated him. I told him that the book I was writing would include a chapter on him, and that we were planning to publish the "bolitas" of his music, and then Fabiola and Lucina sang him the son "El Tecotle" (The Owl). He could not respond verbally, but his daughter said that he nodded and smiled. Within hours, he died.

While filming the California segments of *Pasajero*, Ricardo captured a quote about music from ten-year-old Fabian Melchor at Rancho Betabel in Gilroy. The boy said, in Spanish, "Music is something very special for you and your life. You travel down a road and find a man playing music. You ask him how he learned. You continue on and get older and become what you will be in life, something very special, and until you die, you carry this spirit in your heart and body."

CHAPTER 10

•■•

THE PEDAGOGY OF
INTANGIBLE HERITAGE

In 1995, fifteen-year-old Fabiola Trujillo arrived at Los Cen-zontles Academy. She was born in Oakland but within months had moved to her parents' small pueblo in Zacatecas, where she lived a traditional Mexican life tending to the family milpa alongside her elders. She developed a deep connection to this lifestyle *and* its music, which, for her, are inextrica-bly linked. She wistfully remembers listening to the music of the female duet Las Jilguerillas blasting on the radio while cooking with her grandmother. It was a deep and frightening shock when she returned to the US at the age of seven to live in a ramshackle neighborhood in West Oakland amidst urban chaos and decay. Her memories of her pueblo—reinforced by listening to Mexican music and watching Mexican cinema—protected her sense of self.

Fabiola entered our academy with a determination to sing, but she began by taking guitar classes instead. As her teacher, I grew impatient with her lack of practice and asked her why she was there if she wasn't willing to put in the work. Her friend revealed that Fabiola actually wanted to sing, and so we put her into the singing class. In retrospect, I believe that the reason she didn't initially take the singing class was not only out of shyness but because she was concerned that vocal classes would interfere with how and what she wanted to sing. She was protecting something within her that had become her strength in the face of trauma. Indeed, most vocal techniques taught in schools are not suited for Mexican music, and even in a country with so many people of Mexican origin, there are precious few places where youngsters can learn our artistic traditions. It was already an act of faith for her to take classes with us at all; up until that point, she believed that a person had to be rich or from a family of musicians to have access to training.

Like many children of immigrants, Fabiola helped her parents—her father, Marin, a laborer, and her mother, Maribel, a homemaker—interact with the English-speaking world, and she had to navigate her schooling and extracurricular activities without their guidance. She decorated cakes for her next-door neighbor to earn the money that paid for her braces, and, in time, her income working at Los Cenzontles enabled her to contribute financially to her family and help her parents buy their home. In school, her dyslexia made academic progress difficult, and the poor quality of Richmond schools did not support her needs, passing her from grade to grade with little faith in her ability to learn, but when I hired her to work at Los Cenzontles, it never occurred to me that she would not excel at her job. Commitment and interest are more valuable to me than higher education, and I could see that she was more than capable. It took mutual trust and hard work to make up for her lost schooling, but the result was well worth the investment. As our Academy Program Manager, she has guided generations of students, motivated by her passion for seeing them blossom through the arts. And she has helped their families navigate the various complexities of life faced by immigrants, who trust her because she is also from the neighborhood.

When Alicia Marines, our administrative director, left Los Cenzontles around 1998, I decided that instead of hiring a professional from the outside to replace her, I would invite my students to staff the organization. It was an unusual step, but I needed workers, they needed jobs, and they would work for what I could pay them. None of them had graduated from college, but they had grown up within the program and had a passion for our mission. It was easier for me to train them to work for us than it was to teach outside professionals to value our organizational culture. Mexican revolutionary Emiliano Zapata said that the land belongs to those who work it with their own hands. Similarly, I feel that Los Cenzontles should be led by those who have committed themselves to the work.

When I began to write grants, I quickly learned that philanthropy was laden with unnecessarily opaque jargon, which I had to translate into everyday language that my students would understand. While the task was arduous, it made me a better communicator and kept our work grounded in reality. I believe that if I can't say something in a way that my Mexican grandmother, a highly intelligent woman without a formal education, would understand, it is probably not worth saying. Plus, in this age of social media, learning to speak plainly and concisely is valuable. The same is true in pedagogy. The veneer of snobbery often associated with the arts is usually a smoke screen to disguise mediocrity. After years of working with celebrated artists, I know the difference between meaningful plain speak and the blather of affectation.

Even more, coded language is often used to protect privilege by excluding certain people from accessing power or opportunity. This is especially common in Mexico, where legions of bureaucrats use convoluted language to give an impression of knowledge while numbing the listener into a stupor. My mother used to laugh telling the story of a Mexican professor who was giving a public presentation in Spanish that she was supposed to translate into English. After she translated his long-winded introduction into a few simple sentences, he responded with surprise, "¿Es todo lo que dije?"—"Is that all I said?"

Years ago, I was invited to speak at a scholarly conference on Mexicanidad at an elite Mexico City university. All of the attendees wore name tags indicating their educational status: "Doctor," "Licenciado," or "Señor" in large letters. I was one of only two speakers from the United States, and I had the darkest skin at the entire conference. After presenting my speech in halting Spanish, a Mexican professor congratulated me for "defending" Mexico in the US, but I was *not* there to defend Mexico's cruel caste system, as represented at that conference. I was promoting its people and cultures who would never have been invited there.

The power of class bias alters lives even at a very young age. In our 2008 film *Vivir* (To Live), Hugo Arroyo says, "I think Los Cenzontles has provided a door for the community, for young people to step out of the path that they're supposed to take. When they walk through the doors, they see something that they didn't think was possible, something that maybe their parents or friends said you can't do because you're Mexican, because you're poor, or because you live in San Pablo or Richmond. That's for people who live somewhere else, Hollywood or wherever."

I cringe when I remember the times education advocates have visited our academy and admonished Fabiola and Lucina for not completing college. Promoting higher education is like a mantra that some people mindlessly repeat without considering the feelings of the people they are shaming or the contributions those people might be making. When Fabiola and Lucina took classes at a local community college, they were told that they needed to choose between college and music. We should, of course, encourage young people who wish to pursue higher education, but I believe we should support all young people regardless of their choices or aptitudes. And we must encourage, not discourage, their interests. What is important is that they are contributing something of value and finding meaning in their work.

Creating pedagogy for traditional music born of the working poor required that I unravel layers of class bias that permeate mainstream arts education, which is fundamentally designed to gentrify. Typically, the stories and songs of the working class are filtered, standardized, and contextualized to soften their rough edges. But it is precisely within our traditions' unbridled nature that their inherent power is embedded. My intention is not to romanticize the poverty from which they come but to recognize the fortitude required to lift oneself, and one's family, above the miseries of poverty. There are lessons within the strategies of people in struggle.

Out of respect for our students and our cultural traditions, we have carefully created and cultivated a well-disciplined, unaffected social environment to facilitate deep learning. Activating the power of the arts requires rigor, which is not to be confused with formality. Our classes are also fun and engaging. Nor should we confuse community access with a lack of quality. Too often, youth arts programs in lower-income communities condescend to their students by teaching them to recite boastful slogans that masquerade as self-empowerment but provide them nothing of lasting value. To the contrary, instilling an exaggerated sense of entitlement while denying them the opportunity to learn skills and knowledge is a cruel act of deception. When a child learns to use their hands to create beaded jewelry or master a musical instrument, they are learning to exercise their capacities in a way that cannot be taken from them. Learning the process of learning leads to a lifetime of learning. But this process does not happen in an afternoon, and it cannot be bought or bestowed. It requires years of committed work and access to knowledge, and it is valuable because of the time and effort invested in it.

Rural art forms are traditionally taught over a lifetime within an all-encompassing cultural context. To teach them to students within a modern urban setting, in hourly classes a few days a week, required us to create a hybrid pedagogy. We took what we learned from our folk masters and mixed that with the standard vocal and instrumental techniques available to us, as well as what we knew from our own family practices. In 1995, I hired Timothy Michaels, a trained opera singer who had contracted our kids for an outside recording project, and I spent considerable time with him tailoring his methods to match our music. He provided our students with rigorous vocal training and support, which they fully integrated into the various styles of traditional music they were learning. With this rich body of information, the young members of Los Cenzontles began to create their own unaffected sound and then teach our authentic traditions to new generations of students in a manner that is natural to who they are.

We do not begin by teaching our students to read music, because we've found that having them learn to play by ear better serves the kinds of music that we teach, developing their listening, expression, and groove. In time, they can choose to learn to read notation in private lessons. There *are* styles of music that are best served by reading. But insisting that children read music before playing a musical heritage that is rooted in community cultures with ear-based pedagogy makes little sense. A friend once told me of a young Latino student who came to learn Norteño accordion with him at a community music conservatory. The young man arrived at his first lessons with great enthusiasm, motivated to learn, but was quickly discouraged by the music theory prerequisites and quit soon after. Instead of reading fixed arrangements, our musicians are taught to employ creative ingenuity to fit within a tapestry of sound created alongside those around them.

While we carefully maintain certain core values around pedagogy, I have always tried to be flexible in choosing new styles and repertory. In the mid-1990s, for instance, we had too many girl singers to give each a solo, so I paired them up and delved into Mexico's wonderful dueto repertory, made popular by groups like Las Palomas, Las Hermanas Mendoza, Las Jilguerillas, Las Hermanitas Núñez, and many others. Female duetos were popular during almost every decade of the twentieth century, but they had largely disappeared commercially by the 1990s. Singing in a duet is a great way to learn to listen, phrase together, and blend voices; and the partnership requires significant commitment. I scoured record stores for albums and CDs to find appropriate songs for our students, and we became known for our girl duets, with Fabiola and Lucina eventually becoming our main pairing, though it took a while for them to adjust their voices and personalities to each other. It was, as I suspected, well worthwhile, and they have earned a strong following for their interpretations of rancheras, corridos, pirekuas, boleros, contestadas, and sones, as well as cross-genre songs. They do not try to imitate other groups or the stylings of the past but have instead created a distinctive sound that has kept the repertory in the public eye, forming a bridge to the current resurgence of female duetos in Mexico and the US.

●■●

Lucina Rodriguez and Fabiola Trujillo. Photo by Craig Sherod

In a typical week at Los Cenzontles Academy, we teach classes in music, dance, folk arts, and jewelry in our afterschool program. There is no audition or prerequisite for enrollment. Students must simply be punctual, attend consistently, and be ready to learn. Everyone is challenged to give their best and required to allow others to do the same. The children prepare to perform for recitals and events at which they can share their skills with family and friends.

We accept students starting at the age of five for our beginning movement class. Lucina teaches them games that build listening, movement, and coordination skills. They sing, clap, and use their feet to stomp rhythmic patterns, which eventually become traditional zapateado dance. Incorporating complex rhythms into the body develops the students' balance and rhythm, creating a strong foundation for music learning and preparing them to develop a sense of groove, which is the coveted feel that shapes and defines quality music. Our music and dance students work in teams, and we have our older children mentor the younger ones. All levels of our students practice music and dance together, as we have done since 1989. Fostering this connection between disciplines is invaluable. When music is separated from social dance, tempos tend to speed up and the music loses its feel (which is one of the reasons that swing bands of the 1940s sounded so much better than their revivals: the newer groups didn't have as much opportunity to accompany social dancers). Ry Cooder, whom Linda Ronstadt describes as a master of groove, once told me that every time he encounters Los Cenzontles, he meets a new young person with a great groove, certainly a credit to Lucina's movement classes for children.

Lucina learned to dance with her mother, Baudelia Robles, who would gather her children in the living room of their home near Guadalajara, where they lived with their extended family. When she was eleven, Lucina arrived undocumented in California with her mother and two brothers (while two of her sisters remained in Mexico), joining their father who had been working for years in the US to support them. The family first lived in South Central Los Angeles and then moved to San Pablo, in the Bay Area. The separation from her sisters and her family elders, who were sources of support and strength for her, was traumatic. And the restrictions, stigma, and fear attached to her status as an undocumented immigrant only exacerbated the difficulties lived by many teenagers. But Lucina has always had a bright spark within her, as well as a willful nature that allowed her to protect herself, find community, and exteriorize her struggles.

After Lucina's quinceañera, she began studying at Los Cenzontles at the recommendation of the dance partner with whom she used to enter quebradita competitions. Her musician father, Arturo, told me she was an excellent dancer and suggested

I hire her to teach. I figured that her experience in social dancing would make her a good traditional dancer as well, but she preferred popular music and declined my invitation to take classes. So I made her a deal: she could teach quebradita if she also learned zapateado. She agreed and proved my assumption correct, becoming an excellent traditional dancer and a natural and charismatic teacher who has since taught countless children at Los Cenzontles Academy.

●●●

The traditions that Los Cenzontles teaches are informal in nature, and are usually passed, without institutional support, from generation to generation within families and communities, and across borders. Unless these cultural movements are consumed by the middle class or highly educated, however, they tend to remain unrecognized by the mainstream. But this marginalization also allows these living traditions to keep their inherent free spirit.

One example of a traditional artist who lives mostly off the grid of official folklore is master artist Atilano López Patricio. Every few years, don Atilano travels by bus from his home in Michoacán to the Bay Area to teach his native P'urhépecha traditions to community groups that are willing to learn. He is not supported by the Mexican government or any academic institution, yet he is as good a composer and musician as any other roots artist who performs on large stages. Atilano explains proudly that the P'urhépecha people were never conquered by the Aztecs, their imperialist pre-Columbian rivals, or the Spanish, and I believe that much of their strength comes from their value of art and culture, elements of their society they were cultivating long before the arrival of Spanish colonists. Atilano is generous and open in sharing his talents and knowledge widely; I consider him a *cultural* migrant worker.

Since 1999, don Atilano has taught us his P'urhépecha traditions, lovely and lyrical styles of music that are not as well known
as mariachi or son jarocho. Born into a family of musicians in
the pueblo of Jarácuaro, on one of the islands on Lake Pátzcuaro,
Atilano learned his family traditions from his late father, Gervacio
López, known for creating Danza de los Viejitos. Together in a
gorgeous duet, Atilano and his brother Pedro sing pirekuas, lilt-
ing love songs that Atilano beautifully composes. In the linguis-
tic cadences of their language one can hear the rhythmic origins
of Mexican music. Atilano's family band plays and dances sones
abajeños and thematic danzas on vihuelas, guitars, violins, and
a tololoche string bass. When we featured Atilano in our 2001
Cuatro Maestros tour of California, he was joined by his sons
Roberto and Atilano Jr., who often work as migrant laborers in
the US. The tour also honored Julián González, Andrés Vega and
Mono Blanco, and Santiago Jiménez Jr. and his conjunto tejano,
from San Antonio.

During his visits to California, don Atilano taught
Fabiola and Lucina to sing in the P'urhépecha language, and
our recordings and videos of their beautiful renditions have
earned them a strong online following, as well as respect
from Atilano himself. Although some of their fans believe the
women to be P'urhépecha themselves, we make it clear that
we see Los Cenzontles' connection to Atilano's artistic lineage
(and to those of Mono Blanco and Julián González) not as
one of birthright but as one built on our dedication to artistic
disciplines within the greater Mexican diaspora. In 2022 we
released a film made up of archival video footage from Fabiola
and Lucina's first, and so far only, visit to Atilano's pueblo of
Jarácuaro in 2004. *P'urhépecha Uékani* is a treasured film that
captures don Atilano's family life and the mutual affection
shared between him and the members of Los Cenzontles.

Los Cenzontles with Atilano López Patricio. Photo by Rayna Makizuru

In the mid-1990s, a young woman approached me to help her document danza traditions from Tierra Caliente, Michoacán, as practiced by her family in Redwood City, California. Danzas are lengthy, repetitive rituals based on historical and religious themes and practiced traditionally throughout Mexico. This woman's father's health was failing, and she wanted to document his knowledge while she could. I still regret that I did not have the team or resources at that time to assist, but I never forgot her request, and I have since worked to raise awareness of the value, vibrancy, and power of the participatory arts.

In recent years, there has been increased interest throughout the Mexican diaspora in danzas, which are not focused on the abilities of individual performers but aimed at honoring, with humility, a greater power. I find this exciting and encouraging, as danzas are profound expressions of community culture and a source of spirituality for many. Rampant individualism has brought our society and planet to the psychological and ecological brink, and ultimately we will need to tap into our collective human spirit to light our path forward. Danzas remind us that the power of cultural art, like the power of nature, is greater than any one of us.

In 2002, Julián González taught our musicians and dancers the Danza de los Copetones from his region, in its entirety. He explained the meaning and nuances of the dance movements, and he oversaw the creation of the costumes, with each dancer decorating their own copete, or headpiece, made with bamboo that he had harvested from the on-ramps of local freeways (during which he was once scolded by the California Highway Patrol). We presented the finished danza in all its twelve movements to initiate one of our festivals at the San Pablo Civic Center.

Los Cenzontles has benefited from the influence of so many traditions, including ones brought to us by more recent immigrants from previously remote regions. In the past twenty years, for example, the San Francisco Bay Area has been settled by thousands of people from Xichú, a town in the foothills of the Sierra Madre Occidental range, in the state of Guanajuato. Many of our academy students have parents from this pueblo and were introduced to us by Magda Resendiz, the mother of students Verenice, Favio, and Oswaldo Velazquez. The local Xichú working-class community regularly organizes cultural events called huapangos (a word whose meaning is parallel to fandango), which center around the traditional music, dance, and improvised poetry of the huapango arribeño and son huasteco styles. They invite musicians from around the

Danza de los Copetones, San Pablo Civic Center, 2001. Photo by Armando Quintero

Bay Area, California, and Mexico to come together to celebrate special events or to raise money for community causes, such as medical or burial expenses. In 2016, some of these parents organized a huapango, held in a recreation center in Marin City, to raise funds for Los Cenzontles Academy. These events are dynamic examples of community culture that promote family connections, but even though they fulfill many social and cultural goals of the nonprofit sector in an exemplary manner, they receive no institutional philanthropic support.

Another remarkable cultural phenomenon is the dramatic growth in California of the arpa grande tradition from Tierra Caliente, which I first heard about in Redwood City in the 1990s. In 2014, we met Leonel Mendoza, a talented young harpist with a deep commitment to this tradition from his home region. Remarkably resilient and enterprising, Leonel holds a degree in education and teaches high school, and he can not only play the harp with virtuosity but he can also hunt and butcher large game. Leonel and his brother Victor initially learned to play music from their father, but he was deported when Leonel was fourteen, leaving his sons to be raised in California's Central Valley by their mother and a community of musicians. Because of rampant drug violence in Michoacán in recent years, many musicians from this region have migrated to the US, where they find plenty of work playing for California's immigrant communities. Although they fulfill one of the most important functions in the cultural arts sector—providing entertainment and consolation to the most maligned, and hardest working, people in our society—most will never see a penny of financial support from arts organizations or patrons.

In 2017 we partnered with Leonel to produce the film *Convivencia de Grupos de Arpa Grande, Modesto, CA*. Because of Leonel's deep trust in his community, he was able to convene six arpa grande groups from around Modesto, and our production crew documented this event and released the edited footage as a two-hour film. To date, it has been viewed more than a million times on YouTube, proving the intense interest in this regional tradition on both sides of the border.

In 2014 Los Cenzontles initiated a consultancy program, called Valor Latino, to help nonprofit organizations cultivate relationships with their local Latino communities through locally sourced programming. Lucina led the work to identify existing cultural practices within Mexican immigrant

A still from the film Convivencia de Grupos de Arpa Grande, *Modesto, CA, 2017. Photo by Emiliano Rodriguez*

communities and to build programming around them. One successful example was a partnership with San Geronimo Valley Community Center, in West Marin County. The center sought to forge a deeper relationship with the local Mexican community, many of whom worked the farms and dairies in the area but only interacted with the center as a food bank. Lucina helped the center establish classes for local children in cooking, sewing, and folklórico dance taught by members of their community. Unfortunately, soon after we initiated Valor Latino, the James Irvine Foundation, which had funded the program, divested from arts and culture, leaving this fertile area of work without the resources to continue.

One of the women with whom Lucina worked was Esther Martinez, an elder from Jalisco who was single-handedly responsible for hosting thousands of immigrants from her pueblo of origin when they first arrived in West Marin County to work on its ranches. Now, each December 12, the community hosts an intimate celebration for the Virgin of Guadalupe with a mariachi playing to her image. People whom Esther had helped, and who have since scattered to surrounding cities and towns, come to celebrate La Virgen but also to honor doña Esther, underscoring the direct and powerful connections between community, culture, and gratitude.

For our 2005 album *Los Senn-Sont-Less,* I wrote the song "After All," whose live version closes our 2006 film *Vivir*:

> After all the words were spoken
> And the people all went home
> Still the circle has not broken
> The wheel keeps turning on its own
>
> Thank you for the music
> Thank you for the joy
> Thank you for this time together
>
> See the wonder of our children
> As they learn what they can do
> Hear the memories of our elders
> Of the people that they knew
>
> Thank you for the music
> Thank you for the joy
> Thank you for this time together
>
> Hear the spirit of the ages
> Handed down to us in song
> Hold it close but not too tightly
> So to keep it going strong
>
> Thank you for the music
> Thank you for the joy
> Thank you for this time together

CHAPTER 11

•●•

A GARDEN, NOT A FLOWER STORE

Around the year 2000, Los Cenzontles had five female singers in their late teens: Kristal Gray, Violeta Contreras, Eva Brunner-Velasquez, Fabiola Trujillo, and Lucina Rodriguez. A known Oakland record label approached us to contract two of them to record a Latin album. When I asked which two they wanted, they replied—apparently unaware of or uninterested in the singers' individual voices—"The two thinnest." I let the young women know about the opportunity and they all passed.

I think of the music industry as a flower store where the most profitable parts of a plant are removed from its soil, cut from its roots, and peddled, while the rest is discarded. In contrast, Los Cenzontles is a garden, where all of the elements support the plants and the garden as a whole, and everything is rooted in the same mission and values. Projects that begin as seeds are worked by caring hands and nourished in the fertile soil of our

Los Cenzontles: Fabiola, Lucina, Kristal, Violeta, and Eva, circa 2000. Photo by David Do

organizational culture. We then share the harvest, within our garden and beyond, so that future seeds might be sown.

To pay our faculty, staff, rent, insurance, etc., we raise a small portion of our income from modest class fees, ticketed performances, and merchandise sales, but mostly we rely on donations and grants from people and foundations who recognize the value of our work and whom we consider part of our family. That is why we are a nonprofit organization. Nobody owns us or the work we create. Though there are people who believe that we simply get "free money," we work hard to merit this support, for which we are grateful.

I realize that philanthropy is a daunting challenge, as there is no shortage of need in our complex world. But I believe that providing all children a complete, quality education, which includes the cultural arts, should not even be considered philanthropic but rather a priority social investment. The California Arts Council (CAC), a state agency, supported us with a system of grants that followed our growth during our first eight years. By 2002, the year that the CAC sadly lost all of its granting capacity, its support accounted for 25 percent of our budget. One San Francisco politician who had voted to defund the state agency defended his action by stating that he could not support arts funding while low-income communities lacked basic social services. Couched as concern for the poor, his cynical comment actually revealed his disdain for the poor and working classes, as he had judged them undeserving of such human essentials as the cultural arts. When the government shirks its responsibility to its people, philanthropy is forced to pick up the slack, making resources even more scarce, and putting nonprofits in increased competition with each other.

One of our biggest fundraising challenges has been to piece together support to sustain our holistic long-term vision, in part because philanthropy tends to be project-focused and driven by shorter-term trends. To do this, we needed to figure out ways to convey the work of Los Cenzontles within disparate funding guidelines. From the beginning, our various program areas—classes, events, performances, and productions—have worked together as one organic entity to support our students, like an idyllic Mexican pueblo. This is the most efficient and effective way for us to organize ourselves, but grant guidelines often don't coincide with our methods and vision. For example, one national foundation that was interested in our work only funded programs that exclusively served teens between certain ages. Since most of our families enroll both teens and their younger siblings, we were ineligible to apply. I communicated our cultural circumstances to their program officer, and fortunately within a few years they altered their guidelines and began to fund us. Another problem we have to work around is that some funders only support programs that are offered free of charge; our community members, however, consider our modest fees a sign of mutual respect and accountability. In the 1990s, a local politician told me that a staff person at the county's grant program, which had given us $4,000, threatened to send me to prison for using county funds to make music CDs—a charge that was inaccurate but still unsettling.

I have lost many hours of sleep over the years worrying about making payroll and paying bills (but never failed to do it). Just as importantly, I have been vigilant about protecting the mission and values of the organization. No financial opportunity is worth sacrificing the integrity of our methods. While other nonprofits may prioritize funding over programming and exaggerate their impact, I have never chased money by creating programs specifically to match a grant opportunity, nor have I ever misrepresented our organization. I build fiscal reserves in times of surplus, and I spend them down during years of deficits, without reducing staffing or jeopardizing our impact. Mostly, I rely on the hard work of our team of multitaskers, bound together by a deep commitment to our community and mission, and for whom I do my best to model a strong work ethic. Most of our staff and faculty have been with us for the bulk of their lives, and in return I have made every effort to provide a living wage and opportunities that correspond to their interests. Los Lobos' David Hidalgo, seeing me scurry around during a fundraiser, asked me if I ever rested. My reply was no. In this field, you can't stop working if you're trying to do right by your people.

I respect the value of business. My grandparents built one with vision and hard work. From farmworkers to landscapers to farm owners, they lifted subsequent generations of our family and contributed to the well-being of their community. These days, however, many corporations replace independent businesses, and technology displaces workers. Corporate practices, devoid of social values and community accountability, squander human capacity.

I am deeply concerned about the impact of corporate consumer culture on our children, since it teaches us to hunger for what we want instead of appreciating what we have. It gnaws away at our family and community bonds in order to sell us a sense of belonging, and it convinces us that we are not enough, so we can be sold a sense of worth. It values the clever, sexy gesture that grabs our immediate, and fleeting, attention on social media, while many struggle to find lasting meaning and real human connection.

From an early age, our society teaches children to value the superficial and to mimic provocative movements on expensive, addictive digital devices that provide a hollow sense of accomplishment and that replace, for many, thought, creativity, and actual achievement. Meanwhile, corporations mine our data and monetize our lives and identities while turning our children into marketing memes.

In a society that tries, in countless ways, to convince us to devalue ourselves, the cultural arts can help our children build resourcefulness and resilience that can protect their sense of self. And our ancestral traditions can be of added value *precisely because* our heritage is imprinted with strategies that generations have tapped to find strength and survive trauma. The clues to our identities are more likely to be found in our kitchens, garages, sewing rooms, and record collections than in the Día de los Muertos aisle at a corporate department store.

Children thrive best in secure, communal settings where they learn to socialize within sequential pedagogy, and in my experience, folk culture is an ideal foundation for this type of early arts education. Traditional music, dance, and arts are like cultural stem cells that will support any future musical style the student chooses. Cultural arts encourage them to find their place in a social fabric while exploring the untamed sides of human nature, an important effort when so many other types of education require conformity and linear learning. As a young teen, my son Emiliano referred to this as "allowing my mind to roam free."

One might think that the nonprofit arts sector would have more in common with the garden than the flower store, but that is often not the case. "Selling" our programs to foundations and donors can resemble the marketplace, where community need is the commodity. A major donor once confided that philanthropy can be an exercise in checking boxes, and this means that many nonprofits, instead of expanding the breadth of their missions, lean into their boxes, reinforcing stereotypes about their constituents.

There is a joke that used to circulate about a nonprofit awards ceremony, and it captures the common ways nonprofits stereotyped the communities they served. In the joke, the Asian person is awarded for academics, the African American for sports and music, the Latino for gang prevention, and the Anglo for environmental protection (the "global vision"). Sadly, these perceptions have guided philanthropy for years, and our work has often been judged within these narrow constraints.

In our case, support often came thanks to the instincts of a single foundation program officer who recognized something special about our work and gave us the opportunity to prove our capacity, despite the fact that we did not fit neatly into their guidelines. Over twenty years ago, Melanie Beene, then the program officer at the William and Flora Hewlett Foundation, spent two hours visiting us, sitting with our children in class, seeing far beyond what a grant proposal could convey, and she shepherded us into the foundation's portfolio. Roberta Uno, a program officer in Arts and Creativity at the Ford Foundation, also saw something in our proposal, which had not made the final cut, and she took a chance on us as well. Throughout the decades, we have been fortunate to have received enough support to be able to continue our work. But even after years of advocacy for equitable resourcing, it is still a struggle. Latinos make up almost 20 percent of America's population (and 70 percent of that 20 percent are of Mexican origin), but between 2009 and 2019 only 1.3 percent of philanthropic dollars supported Latino-based organizations, according to the Oakland nonprofit organization Hispanics in Philanthropy. And to make things worse, many Bay Area foundations are choosing to divest from arts and culture in general.

Once you understand the biases with which Latinos are viewed by mainstream society, you can see these same biases reflected in philanthropy. One common perception is that our families are viewed as fundamentally flawed and incomplete. Latino men are often perceived as machos who subjugate women, and so scholarships for young Latinas have become a philanthropic priority, with the subtext being that they must be saved from the dysfunction of their family cultures. But then where does that leave our boys? We would be better off seeking holistic strategies that recognize our wholeness rather than creating a patchwork of programs based on bias.

The three children of Odilon Velázquez—Sarahi, Miriam, and Andres—have attended our academy for over fifteen years. Raised on the small ranch of Cieneguilla, Guanajuato, Odilon, a soft-spoken maintenance worker, plays guitar and sings in a lovely Mexican country style. He teaches neighborhood children from the family's home in the Canal District of San Rafael, a Latino neighborhood, and he plays music at church. I admire his music making, and while his kids are in class we sometimes practice and make videos of our duets. His children also attended another music enrichment program for young people of color, and I remember once seeing a promotional video for the organization in which they claimed to provide music to children who had no music in their homes—a statement that struck a nerve because, at that very moment, the screen was showing Odilon with one of his daughters. I sent an email to the executive director of that organization to inform them that their students do indeed have musical culture in their homes, but I received no response. Portraying families of color as "incomplete" to donors may be a successful fundraising strategy, but it harms our community by propagating false deficit-driven stereotypes.

The director of a national foundation once described philanthropy as capitalism's runoff, catering to the interests of the wealthy instead of focusing on need and opportunity. The kinds of donors who seek to enhance their social status by contributing to, for instance, a prestigious symphony or museum are not likely to support a Mexican American cultural center for low-income children housed in a tattered strip mall. While gifts to low-income communities—driven by pity for the underserved—often aim to assuage the guilt of privilege, I am not interested in provoking anyone's guilt or pity, feelings that can be tragically counterproductive and that reinforce the very societal biases within which inequity festers. I prefer to see our work as a collaborative effort to which all kinds of people can contribute what they have, whether it is vision, labor, talent, or resources.

A few years ago we were considered for a substantial monetary prize for exemplary music education programs for underserved youth. The proposal asked how our work effected system change, and we answered as well as we could. As a finalist, we hosted a site visit for the philanthropist and his staff at which our teachers would discuss our work and our students would perform. Linda Ronstadt even came to speak on our behalf. After the meeting start time came and went, however, we heard that the rideshare driver of the philanthropist had gotten lost. Our efforts to direct the driver failed, and the man was left stranded at a nearby Starbucks, frustrated and intent on canceling his visit. His staff members stood there paralyzed while Fabiola and Lucina jumped in a car to fetch the donor, who finally submitted to their repeated appeals to come to our facility. Once here, he spent another twenty minutes brooding while we all, including Linda, tried to reanimate him.

Our neighborhood was built to be unstable, due to its geographic vulnerability, poor home construction, polluted air quality from nearby oil refineries, and fragile infrastructure, all of which create a constant buzz of insecurity that threatens its inhabitants' sense of well-being. Even more daunting is the pervasive mindset that allows for such inequities to persist, as though poor and working-class people *deserve* the indignities of poverty in order to motivate them to strive for greater wealth. To me, it is obviously unreasonable to expect small nonprofit organizations to change vast systems of inequity—especially when we are dependent on the capricious nature of wealth in America, which itself is part of the systemic problem.

●●●

To stay in touch with community sentiment, I often solicit opinions from the people at Los Cenzontles on various subjects. Once, I asked Fabiola and Lucina what abuses they were most against: Those based in racism, gender bias, domestic violence, or what? Their answer was simply, "We are against abuse," spoken with the common sense of the working class. The overwhelming, and revolving, number of priority causes in the philanthropic zeitgeist, all of them created at a safe distance from communities in need, can be paralyzing. But lip service and newly minted jargon does little real-world good and usually just reinforces existing bias. In my opinion, lasting solutions are simple, elegant, and based on actual work. We are better off using our limited time and energy serving our communities rather than repeating buzzwords within the nonprofit echo chamber.

I have developed a reputation among foundations for speaking candidly about our needs and challenges. While this could be considered risky because it might appear ungrateful, I see frank communication as a sacred responsibility and a demon-stration of my gratitude and commitment to the field. We are all part of the same ecosystem, so if we don't share our truth, nothing will improve.

Los Cenzontles effectively represents our community because it is run by people, including artists, *from* our community, and who share a long-held passion for our vision. I believe that the cultural arts would be better served by promoting a diversity of organiza-tional systems that directly represent our cultural communities. I have been concerned about the emergence of a "professionalized" arts sector driven by businesspeople (at the expense of artists) who typically staff organizations in revolving three-year stints, focused on building their resumes while the organization's mission and impact wobbles. This approach diminishes both community arts visions and community artists, and it has contributed to growing inequity and gentrification in the field, favoring major arts insti-tutions—which are already structured like corporations—that absorb the lion's share of philanthropic resources. I believe that nonprofits, which are mission based, can help counterbalance some of our societal inequities created by corporatism, and that is why it is so important to promote not only values-based projects but also the native practices that support them.

In 2020 we embarked on a strategic planning process to increase our organization's sustainability, a term that has come to mainly imply money. But sustainability is actually rooted in the balance of organizational attributes that also include an engaged staff and relevant programming. As is typical, the arts manage-ment consultant we hired began the process by congratulating us for our long history of success and then advised us to change and adopt standard business strategies. He suggested, for example, that I spend less time playing music with our young people and more time as a consultant to other agencies, which is lucrative. But working with kids and music motivates me! Consulting does not. Making a lot of money is an intoxicating promise, but I have learned from experience that the cost of its blind pursuit is dangerously shortsighted because it siphons energy away from mission, organizational culture, and community: the true lifeblood of our work. I believe that we are more likely to achieve sustainability by pursuing our passions rather than abandoning them.

I tried mightily to convince the consultant to find a creative hybrid solution with us that respected Los Cenzontles' practices, which are proven to work. Meeting each other halfway is what musicians do when we collaborate: we accommodate, and build on, each other's voices. But the consultant's own business model prohibited him from spending that kind of time with us. It seemed to me that his mandate was to sell us a high-priced, off-the-shelf product and then move on to his next client.

The consultant also confided that he felt that Latino arts leaders spent too much time debating identity descriptors while white leaders spent their time raising money. In saying this, he laid bare one of America's most corrosive myths: that social inequity results from minority dysfunction, which could be remedied if only we all behaved more like white businessmen. Before 2016, I probably would have overlooked his comment as clumsy and misinformed, but given the bigotry unleashed within our country in recent years, I could not let it go. So, I replied that if white leaders spent more time discussing identity and less time on the pursuit of money, our country might not be at the precipice of democratic collapse. He did not respond. Because his proposals clashed with our values so starkly, especially while we were navigating the painful challenges of COVID-19, we terminated the consultancy and finished the process ourselves.

CHAPTER 12

●◗●

DAVID HIDALGO

When talking about his approach to creativity, David Hidalgo quotes the title of "Weird Al" Yankovic's song "Dare To Be Stupid." I take this advice to heart in every aspect of my work, as learning, growing, and creative expression all require risk. If we operate within the safety of convention, we will never transcend it. For a young person, and especially a teenager, taking the risk to express themselves can be terrifying. Risk, I tell my students, requires faith, which is an invisible bridge between what you know and what you don't yet know. To get to the other side, you must cross the bridge, and if you don't cross, you will not learn. During a recent recording session, thirteen-year-old Natalie Caldera, relatively new to singing, became nervous when it was her turn to record her voice. Her eyes watered and her voice shook, but she gathered her courage, followed her training, and sang with clarity and strength. These are lessons, embedded in experience, that will serve a young person for a lifetime. Indeed, David has created joy and beauty through music by taking risks—pushing the limits of his creativity to vividly capture moments in time.

David was still in junior high school when he met the friends who would become Los Lobos, whose remarkable journey continues to this day. Each member contributes something essential to the band's powerful sound and body of work, and their longtime relationships have kept them grounded. But for me, it is the fountain of David's musical imagination that has lifted the group to such great artistic heights. He has both the humility to recognize his limitations and the confidence to stretch them when there is something he wants to say. His goal is not simply to shine light on his own brilliance but to expose something in the music that touches him. And along the way he encourages others to step into the spotlight as well. His artistic career has revealed him to be a man of the world, but the essence of his heartfelt vision is his identity as a Chicano from East Los Angeles.

You don't have to be Mexican American to appreciate David's gifts. Having played the music of many cultures, he has collaborated with artists such as Bob Dylan, Robert Plant, Tom Waits, Dolly Parton, Elvis Costello, and many others, both famous and not. He has also participated in a number of side projects, including, most notably, the innovative Latin Playboys and Los Super Seven, with both of whom he has recorded two albums each. And with Los Cenzontles, he has (so far) recorded five full albums, participated on three more, and cut a number of singles and videos.

Los Lobos represents Mexican American culture boldly, without kitsch or pretense. For this they have been both rewarded and punished. Instead of riding the coattails of their 1987 mega-hit cover of "La Bamba" by releasing a follow-up project in the same vein, their next album was *La Pistola y El*

Corazón (1988), an exquisite collection of acoustic songs in various traditional Mexican genres. Tellingly, though the group has been together for fifty years and is respected by the music industry and fans alike, they have not yet been inducted into the Rock and Roll Hall of Fame, a detail that may seem insignificant in the face of their enduring contribution to American culture but that says something important about the status of Mexican Americans in our society. If a band as impactful as Los Lobos can be overlooked by the music industry, what does that bode for the rest of us?

In 2005, eleven years after our *Papa's Dream* recording sessions, I heard that Los Lobos was looking for a Mexican brass banda to join the belated California tour for their celebrated album *Kiko*, which was originally released in 1992. I replied to the call, offering an abbreviated version of our Banda Los Cenzontles that included Hugo Arroyo on sousaphone, Tom Fuglestad and Felipe Leon on trumpets, Hector Espinoza and Jorge Cruz on clarinets, Cristian Rodriguez on tarolas, and me on the big tambora bass drum. Toward the end of each concert, we joined Los Lobos for "Rio de Tenampa," sung by David, and for encores "Carabina .30-30" and "Volver, Volver," sung by Cesar Rosas. Our original Los Cenzontles member Angel Abundez also played harp on "Saints Behind the Glass," sung by Louie Pérez. I will forever associate the opening drum introduction of "Done Gone Blue"—played with a powerful, soulful groove by Cougar Estrada—as our cue to get ready. Being side players on commercial gigs is never too comfortable a place to be in the music industry, which is dominated by a "kiss up and kick down" ethic, but the members of Los Lobos went out of their way to treat us with kindness. After one venue gave us a stairwell to use as our green room, David, who saw us eating dinner on the stairs under fluorescent lights, invited us into the plush lounge to eat with them.

At that time, Los Cenzontles had been recording and touring various genres of traditional music and we were now ready to create more original music. Hugo was writing rock songs, and Lucina was exploring Latin pop with diverse rhythms for her compositions. So, while it seemed like a long shot, I began to look for ways to get closer to David in order to invite him to mentor the group. Treating him with distant respect only seemed to stiffen him up, but joking around, which is my default when I am relaxed, turned out to be the key. I soon realized that his sense of humor was similar to my dad's, and I wondered if that came from the fact that, like my father, he had spent his early years growing up in Central Los Angeles before moving to East LA. Dave's father sold caskets, and the family lived above the warehouse for a time. I can only imagine the kinds of adventures he and his older brothers had playing among the coffins, which is perhaps one of the reasons that his imagination is as active as it is.

We did not have the financial resources to pay his professional fees, so, in asking him to work with us, we were relying on his generosity in more ways than one. My persistence eventually paid off, and he agreed to come up to record with us in 2007. For the first hour of his visit, a friend of his remained close by to make sure everything was okay, but at a certain point, while we were messing around, Dave suddenly blurted out to me, "Man, you're a brother!" and let his friend go. He then told me that there was no need for us to rent him a car because he would spend his days within our care. So, amidst our comfortable couches, reclining chairs, warm homemade or take-out meals, stories, and jokes, we stretched out and made music. We began recording each day around noon and ended around midnight (or later), staying flexible, following everyone's energy levels.

During those three days of recordings, we captured a thrilling exploration of sounds and grooves, ranging from explosive rock, freewheeling instrumental road trips, and new takes on old traditions. Dave played nearly every guitar in the building at some point, listening for something special inside of each one, and he seemed pleased to be back in a Mexican neighborhood with people who lovingly honored our roots while testing their limits. I had a list of prepared songs, to which we freely made substitutions—for instance, sitting down to record a classic ranchera but then suddenly migrating to a long freeform jam. Some of the more obscure folk rhythms could puzzle him for a moment, but he seemed to enjoy the challenge and always rose to meet it. Sometimes we would fuse styles, as we did with the venerable ranchera "Mi Unico Camino," which is typically played in a 3/4 rhythm. We played it in 6/8 with a strong back-beat and gave it a roadside honky-tonk feel. Dave jerry-rigged a bottleneck to use as a slide for his guitar and accompanied Fabiola and Lucina's rich, soulful duet.

David Hidalgo in Los Cenzontles' studio. Photo by Mike Melnyk

Dave is very sensitive to human energy, so we made sure to give him plenty of space. I remember seeing him backstage right before the Los Lobos *Kiko* show at the Hard Rock Cafe on LA's

Sunset Boulevard, looking for a place to hide from the throngs of music industry people. Professionally, he is often asked to recreate a certain sound he is known for, but while he was with us, I just wanted him to enjoy his time, so we did not crowd him with expectations. Perhaps the space and support we provided is why, at one point, he stood up in the middle of our large room and exclaimed, "I feel so free!"

During one session that went past midnight, when we were all ready to stop for the day, I asked if we could record one more song. I suggested we do a version of the classic bolero "Creí"— also popular as a Chicano oldie—but in a way that would capture the late-night mood of a band playing to an emptying neighborhood nightclub. Dave tweaked his guitar slightly out of tune and played an incredibly poignant solo, weaving sublime and delicate beauty amidst the imaginary smell of stale beer. When trying to figure out which musicians would overdub the song's melody, he suggested the Estrada Brothers, a Chicano jazz ensemble composed of veteranos Ruben Estrada, Henry Estrada, and Henry Nava (respectively the father, uncle, and family friend of Lobos drummer Cougar Estrada) on vibes and saxophones. One afternoon, Hugo Arroyo and I traveled to Southern California to record them, and while driving through the crop fields of Camarillo, in Ventura County, the smell of fertile soil evoked powerful memories of my grandma's farmland. I felt that I was not just capturing the sounds of venerable musicians but also sweet memories of my childhood.

The sessions became our 2008 album *Songs of Wood & Steel*, which was met with great critical acclaim. One of its tracks, "Howling Moon," was composed by Hugo Arroyo, with Dave's guidance, in the style of a fusion son jarocho. I later wrote lyrics based on a candid moment during the recording session when Dave, Lucina, and Fabiola stood in our parking lot gazing at the full moon.

Howling at the ceiling, thinking of the sky,
Remember the feeling, what it was to cry.

Songbird went out flying way beyond his home,
Wasn't scared of dying, didn't feel alone.

Did you see the face or rabbit on the moon?
Light that came down shining ended all too soon.

We often think of virtuoso musicians as standing out above the rest, but the truly great ones distinguish themselves by listening to others around them and finding their place within the music. During one of our sessions, marveling at Dave's ability, I told him, "You're so damned talented." He replied, uncharacteristically stern, "C'mon, man, don't lay that trip on me." I think I understood what he was telling me. He wanted to be among us, not cast apart. Not everyone can be as brilliant as he is, but we can all become ourselves, though there are many forces in the world that try to inhibit us from doing so. I believe that working to develop one's own authentic voice is among the most important goals of the arts, an effort that might help us avoid getting lost in the confusion of social pretense and manipulation. And then, if we can join our voices to those of others, maybe we can connect meaningfully, and perhaps transcend the moment.

Sometimes I like the feeling of being lost on a car ride, even when I am not far from home, because it allows me to see something familiar in a new way. Working with Dave taught me to keep trusting my musical instincts and to follow them where they lead. He once said that Los Cenzontles was not like most LA music groups, who play neatly within stylistic boundaries; he assumed that our fluidity was due to Jerry Garcia's influence on the Bay Area and Northern California. I don't know if that is true, but I know that his visit validated us and ignited our creative imaginations, and well after he left, the ceiling of our humble storefront seemed to have risen another twenty feet.

I think of David Hidalgo as a kind of Everyman, and his genius does not change that. There is genius within people all around us, but what distinguishes him is that he has found a way to make a place for himself in the music industry, and not through self-promotion but through his musical honesty and generosity. It's his Everyman essence that makes his music resonate, as if he also speaks for the invisible.

For those who live in society's shadows, I wrote verses about the tenuous protection that invisibility provides us in a predatory world. I recited them to Dave during a break in one of our recording sessions, and he immediately got up, walked to the studio, dialed in a heavy sound on the guitar amp, established a groove, and gestured chord changes to the other musicians as we recorded "Invisible Man" in one take.

> Invisible man, keep your head down low
> Your invisible head is beginning to show
> Invisible man
> Invisible man
>
> Just like you've done five hundred years
> Mouth shut tight, satellite ears
> Invisible man
> Invisible man
>
> Don't look now, they're talking 'bout you
> Invisible man, what you gonna do?
> Invisible man
> Invisible man

Invisible man, what you gonna do?
Invisible man, I'm invisible too
Invisible man
Invisible man

We have continued to collaborate with David in a number of ways, mining our shared musical interests during performances, travels, and recordings. He has supported our work by playing at benefits, and he has introduced us to many great musicians, including Taj Mahal, Pete Sears, Raul Malo, and Elvin Bishop. Our friend and supporter Robert Mailer Anderson, an author and lifelong fan of Los Lobos, hosted a fundraising event at his Pacific Heights home for Los Cenzontles that featured David Hidalgo, Dave Alvin, Flaco Jiménez, Pete Sears, Max Baca, and Los Cenzontles. Robert also invited David to record his song "Inside of Us All" for his 2019 film *Windows on the World*, which is about a migrant family caught up in the events of 9/11. Robert cast me in a speaking role alongside its star, Edward James Olmos, whom I first saw on the Mark Taper Forum stage as the character El Pachuco in a 1978 production of *Zoot Suit.* Acting with him was both thrilling and frightening. David attended a screening of the film in Los Angeles and told me afterward that he partially covered his eyes when I appeared on screen, saying that he didn't want to see a friend screw up. Luckily I didn't, and for that he congratulated me.

Throughout the years, Dave has returned to our academy many times, and he seems to especially enjoy playing with young musicians. During one of those appearances, I remember seeing three-year-old Belinda Ortega in her father's arms, intensely watching and listening to Dave play the accordion. Now Belinda is a fifteen-year-old who plays multiple instruments with remarkable confidence and expressivity. I can only imagine what influence David Hidalgo's ongoing presence in her life has had on her. For Los Cenzontles, and the world, his contributions are immeasurable.

CHAPTER 13

●●●

CROSSING CULTURAL RIVERS

Though Mexico has always been part of the world, its deep historic connections are not often recognized; and while people of Mexican origins have lived on these lands since long before the United States existed, Mexican Americans are routinely treated as if we do not belong. Mainstream media ignores and segregates our music, excluding it from World Music and Americana playlists. And though Mexican musicians informed the birth of jazz, and Mexican vaqueros invented cowboys—both quintessential American cultural icons—our contributions remain hidden. This is not trivial. Denying us our place and shared history makes it easier to cast us as the Other, rendering us vulnerable to scapegoating.

I have found that the deeper we dig into our Mexican roots the more we find them tangled with the roots of others, and I believe that connecting with the roots of others reinforces our own. Here in the Bay Area, we live our daily lives alongside people from many backgrounds. In my neighborhood, our Mexican market is owned by Yemeni people who speak Arabic, English, and Spanish to their Latino, white, Arab, African American, and Asian customers. America's myth of racial purity insists that, at its core, we are a "white country," within which racial and ethnic groups exist on the periphery. But people of all backgrounds have always directly interacted with each other through business, marriage, and shared customs. The true fabric of America is, and always has been, interwoven. But that is not reflected in popular culture.

The 2008 economic crisis dried up financial support for our touring opportunities, which was ultimately for the best, as we could not leave our academy for long periods of time since our performers were also our teachers. So, I sought other projects that we could do closer to home, which included more traditional and cross-cultural explorations through recordings and films. I remembered that when David Hidalgo first entered our academy to record *Songs of Wood & Steel*, he looked around, clearly impressed, and said, "Taj needs to see this." And then he asked, "Does Queen Ida still live around here?"—referring to the legendary zydeco accordionist who had lived and performed in Richmond. Dave is a man of few words, but they pack a punch, and indeed within a few years we would record the albums *American Horizon*, with blues great Taj Mahal, and *Shades of Brown*, which fused Latin music with African American and Creole traditions.

American Horizon is a concept album about migration from both Mexican American and African American perspectives. Los Cenzontles was joined by Dave and Taj, who is most commonly celebrated for his blues music, though he is versed in music of many world cultures. Taj, with deep knowledge of Mexican music, has long been connected to Chicano musicians, and he stood alongside Cesar Chavez in the 1970s to support the United Farm Workers.

For the album, which was funded by a Creative Work Fund grant, I wanted to tell a musical story about a young person leaving their home—either a Mexican ranch or a Southern farm—to seek opportunity beyond the horizon, whether that be over the US–Mexico border or the Mason–Dixon line. On a large sheet of paper that we hung in the academy's reception area, I mapped out a narrative arc, with points along the way that we would match with new or traditional songs. They included an opening dream, the departure, a first encounter with a new land, seeking romance, work, disillusionment, a test of faith, resolution through gratitude, and redemption through celebration. For six days, we created and recorded grooves and song forms for each section of the journey.

Our stellar rhythm section included Los Lobos drummer Cougar Estrada, Taj's drummer Kester Smith, and Cuban percussionist Carlos Caro. My son Emiliano, then sixteen years old, was becoming an excellent bass player, and he joined us with confidence beyond his years, paying close attention to the mastery that surrounded him. Hugo Arroyo played bass and jarana and sang and composed the inventive work song "Overtime." His vocal rendition of "Carpintero," serving our narrative as a secular prayer, was accompanied by me and Dave on tenor guitarras de son and is among the most heartfelt recordings of the traditional son jarocho "El Pájaro Carpintero."

After a week of creating instrumental tracks, our guests went home, entrusting me to write melodies and lyrics to many of the original songs. Once that was done, Taj, Dave, Hugo, Fabiola, Lucina, and I added lead vocals. I came up with bilingual lyrics for a blues shuffle Taj had written to capture the impressions of our rural migrant first seeing the big city. I will never forget Taj's face when he heard Fabiola and Lucina's brilliant chorus on "Sueños" (Dreams). He was thrilled and I was relieved.

Luces de neón (neon lights)
    Shining bright
Sus colores (their colors)
    Fill the night
Autopistas (freeways)
    Moving fast
Trocas grandes (big trucks)
    Built to last

Sueños

La discoteca (the disco)
    Gonna dance
Apretadito (holding tight)
    Sure romance
Chicas lindas (pretty girls)
    Looking fine
Las güeritas (the fair-skinned ones)
    Will be mine

Sueños

La lotería (the lottery)
    I gotta play
La ruleta (roulette)
    Win today
Casa nueva (new house)
    Swimming pool
Buena chamba (good job)
    No one's fool

Sueños

Like *Songs of Wood & Steel* had been two years before, *American Horizon* was met with critical acclaim and was embraced by respected artists. In an editorial about the album for the *New York Times*, journalist Lawrence Downes wrote, "It both honors and upends traditional Mexican music, tapping deep roots as it flowers into something completely new, and distinctly American. . . . It's a new song, and an old story—the perfect fit for a country that has been renewed by immigration, but also perplexed and sometimes frightened by it. Some have declared the surge in immigrant Spanish-speakers as the end of America as we know it. But as *American Horizon* shows, it's just another new beginning."

Taj Mahal with Los Cenzontles, 2013. Photo by Craig Sherod

●●●

In 2014 I looked up local zydeco accordionist Queen Ida, hoping to collaborate on a Latin zydeco project. One of the groups that had settled in Richmond to work its shipyards during World War II were Creole people from Louisiana, who brought along their food and culture. In fact, Richmond was the West Coast capital of zydeco music for years. By the time I got in touch with her, Queen Ida was already retired and living on the San Francisco peninsula, but we found a worthy heir in Creole accordionist Andre Thierry, living just a few blocks from Los Cenzontles Academy. Although they did not know each other at the time, Andre and Lucina had attended Helms Middle School in San Pablo together. For decades, Andre's grandmother Lena Pitre had organized dances for the once-thriving Creole community at St. Mark's Church in Richmond, presenting such notable musicians as Clifton Chenier, Geno Delafose, and Queen Ida. This same social hall now hosts folk music events for the Mexican community of Xichú, Guanajuato, attended by many of our students' families.

Shades of Brown is a reunion of our shared cultural history, mixing rubboard, percussive zapateado, and conga drums on popular and traditional covers as well as on original songs sung in English, Spanish, and French Creole. Dave Hidalgo's bright, rich voice and searing guitar are featured on our cover of the swamp pop classic "Mathilda" (written by Andre's great uncle Hugo Thierry, of Cookie and His Cupcakes), and he is backed by our full eleven-piece Mexican banda, arranged by Hector Espinoza. Lucina wrote an original song, "Fin de Semana," for the album as a banda cumbia with a zydeco twist, in reminiscence of her days as a young teenager dancing quebradita.

I wrote the song "Riding to the Water" thinking of Richmond's hills overlooking bay waters, and its streets full of rich cultural connections that remain invisible to most of us.

> In the darkness of the shadows that surround
> There is love between us
> And though the light is often nowhere to be found
> There are moments that redeem us

In the spaces of the silence that divide
There's a song between us
And when we're muted by the loneliness inside
It's the music that relieves us

Ruben Moreno, at the concert for Shades of Brown *at Los Cenzontles, 2014. Photo by Mike Melnyk*

On the last day of the recording session, we quickly transitioned our space back into a theater and hosted a concert for a packed audience of Latinos, Creoles, and others, as well as special attendees Linda Ronstadt and Bonnie Raitt. Andre's colleague Ruben Moreno, part Creole and part Chicano, who had been playing rubboard in the studio without theatrics, surprised us all with his explosive onstage antics during "I Got Loaded," an R&B classic composed by Lil' Bob from Louisiana and famously covered by Los Lobos. Unaware of his dynamic stage persona, I had placed him in the back row with percussionists Cougar Estrada, Sydney Pennie, and Carlos Caro. After the show, Linda told me that I should have put him up front. If I had known, I would have! Nevertheless, the show was electric, and even after the audience left, Lucina, Andre, and the other younger members of the collaboration continued to share dance moves in our parking lot.

Finding common grooves between zydeco and Latin rhythms was not difficult, and it was a joy to explore the many living musical connections between Louisiana, Mexico, and the Caribbean. Kristal Gray, a Cenzontles alumna who was with us between the ages of eight and twenty, was a mix of African American, Native American, Cuban, and Mexican, and she could sing a soul classic or a Mexican ranchera equally well, plus dance son jarocho with the best of them. Most people assumed she was simply African American, but I have learned that few people are simply anything. We all have fascinating, connected lineages.

●●●

In 2009, we participated on *San Patricio*, an album that was by Ry Cooder and legendary Irish folk group the Chieftains and that also featured a stunning roster of Mexican musicians including Los Tigres del Norte, Chavela Vargas, and Linda Ronstadt. It was an ingenious mashup of Irish and Mexican music telling the story of the St. Patrick's Battalion, composed of Irish American conscripts who were sent to fight against Mexico in 1849 but instead changed sides and were later hanged by the Americans. Mexicans and Irish both share a passion for 6/8 rhythms, nostalgic themes, Catholicism, and distilled spirits.

It was fascinating to observe the album's masterminds—Ry together with Paddy Moloney—in the studio, each with a very different musical approach but with a shared reverence for tradition and respect for tradition bearers. I was taken aback by how loudly they listened to the sessions in the control room, as if they needed to feel the music in their bodies in addition to hearing it. Ry, whose good advice on song selections I have enjoyed many times, once told me that music making was problem solving, an insight that has helped me refine my productions.

For the album, we recorded a Mexican-Irish version of a mariachi son abajeño we had learned from Julián González: "El Chivo" (The Goat), about an animal venerated in both Mexican and Irish cultures. The album also took its theme from a movement from Danza de los Copetones that Julián had taught us. With the Chieftains and Ry, Los Cenzontles toured California, Scotland, and Ireland, along with an amazing cast of musicians and dancers. One morning of the tour, I teasingly answered Paddy's phone call saying, in a terrible imitation of an Irish brogue, "Top o' the morning to you, Paddy." He cracked up and later sang me the lyrics of an old commercial jingle to the tune of "The Mexican Hat Dance" that had once been popular in Ireland. At the 2009 Celtic Connections festival at the Glasgow Royal Concert Hall in Glasgow, Scotland, we performed side by side with Ry, Paddy, the Chiefs, and their guest artists. In front of us were a gaggle of Irish dancing girls, and behind was an army of Scottish bagpipers, a thunderous sound that I will never forget!

When we toured Cuba in 2016 to shoot our documentary *Conexiones, A Cuban-Mexican Connection*, the last thing I wanted to do was make another film about the Cuban Revolution or the Cold War, themes that usually eclipse the many other stories deserving to be told about the Cuban people and their remarkable cultural history. So instead we explored the enduring love affair between Cubans and Mexicans, which I first learned about in 2002 when we recorded two Mexican tracks (with clear African influences) with legendary Afro-Cuban rumberos Lázaro Ros, Gregorio "El Goyo" Hernández Ríos, and Roberto Borrell.

During a brief respite in US–Cuban animosity, Los Cenzontles performed Mexican music in four cities down the spine of the center of the island. Foreign groups rarely get permission to tour within Cuba, so people were attentive to our presentations and grateful for our visit. The trip and film were sponsored by our dear friend and supporter Jonathan Logan, with whom we have shared many great adventures. Another friend and supporter, Rick Swig, had shared his many connections in Cuba that cut through red tape and paved the way for our trip. Jon, his party, and Rick joined us as we traveled in an air-conditioned bus to our various locations, with a driver and a guide, to collaborate with Cuban musicians that represented different layers of Cuba's musical society. These included: La Familia Miranda in Las Tunas, whose music represented their rural, family lifestyle and identity; the performance-ready amateur musicians and dancers in Sancti Spíritus performing show music, including two Cuban men dressed in mariachi charro outfits singing popular rancheras to prerecorded instrumental tracks; a community dance group dedicated to Mexican ballet folklórico in Santa Clara; and internationally celebrated jazz musicians playing at a Havana garden reception for our visit.

The resulting film is a tour de force, shot, recorded, and edited by James Hall, who describes it as a "pure" documentary, meaning we had no idea what conditions or situations we would encounter but just captured what we could on the fly. We crafted the storylines on the bus and in hotel lobbies, using revelations we made along the way.

In 2018, having already visited Veracruz and Cuba, we were finally able to visit the third corner of the historic cultural triangle that is Veracruz, Cuba, and New Orleans by spending a weeklong residency in NOLA at Preservation Hall, staying two blocks from Frenchmen Street. We met wonderful musicians and community members, many of whom were knowledgeable about Mexico's cultural connections to New Orleans, where a statue of Mexico's former president Benito Juárez stands in remembrance of the two times, during the 1850s, he lived there in exile. In exchange for that hospitality, he later invited free people of color from Louisiana to settle in Mexico when conditions became difficult for them at home. The NOLA–Mexico connection was renewed in 2005 as workers from Mexico flocked to the city to rebuild after Hurricane Katrina, and many of them never left, instead joining their new community and contributing to the cultural mix that defines the region. As much as some people might wish it, history and culture never stop evolving.

On that trip, perhaps our most moving encounter was with a group of women at Ashé Cultural Arts Center who dance African rhythms for healing. We performed for them and they for us, and then we formed a circle to talk, play, and dance together. I was deeply touched by their expressions of solidarity for the children who were languishing in cages at the US–Mexico border at that time. I thought of the many people who pit Latinos and African Americans against each other to enhance their own power, and I was reminded of why we must always speak directly to people from other communities, rather than allowing outside groups with their own agendas to interject themselves between us. What we have in common is much stronger than what divides us.

Los Cenzontles with the Preservation Hall All-Stars, New Orleans, 2018.
Photo by James Hall

Also in 2018, Los Cenzontles released our album *A la Mar*, featuring early-music violinist Shira Kammen, who made this a collaboration that crossed not only cultures but time itself. The foundation of much of Mexico's folk music comes from Europe's medieval, Renaissance, and Baroque music, all of which Shira specializes in. With this background in mind, recording sones jarochos, sones huastecos, and alabanzas was a profoundly satisfying exploration. Shira, with whom I have worked since the 1990s, is the rare musician who has not only impeccable technique and an accurate historical performance practice but also an open spirit and a genius for improvisation. She had previously joined Los Cenzontles on other tracks, including our covers of Neil Young's "Cortez the Killer," alongside David Hidalgo, and our version of Jimi Hendrix's "Little Wing," which appears on our 2016 *Covers* album, which featured Latin versions of American popular music.

Another cross-cultural project that is close to my heart is our bilingual recording of the cowboy standard "Red River Valley," a song my father used to sing to me and my brother as children. Pedal steel master Ed Littlefield, a supporter of our work, joined old-timey musicians Laurie Lewis and Tom Rozum in creating a Mexican cowboy version with me and Emiliano accompanying Fabiola and Lucina singing Spanish-language lyrics that I wrote for the chorus.

> Si me amas ven a mi lado
> No te apures en decirme adiós
> Y recuerda aquel lindo valle
> Y al vaquero que tanto te amó
>
> Come and sit by my side if you love me
> Do not hasten to bid me adieu
> And remember that Red River Valley
> And the cowboy who loved you so true

The cultural history of humankind is a tangled web that we will never fully be able to unravel, much of it having been lost to time. However, the vast cultural legacy that exists leaves us a great deal to work with, especially if we view it with an informed, open mind. It has been my great privilege to be able to work with kindred spirits from a wide variety of backgrounds. Within the music of our world is a profound reservoir of human spark, fed by countless individuals over time immemorial whom we will never know but who nevertheless helped create the path upon which we travel. There are few greater connections than that.

CHAPTER 14

●●●

STATE OF SHAME

Amidst the incessant shriek of marketers in our power-driven society, the humble go largely unnoticed. Yet they live, contribute, and create, all the while bearing the brunt of society's cruelest inequities. In our neighborhood, the high price of housing forces working families to share small, fragile homes and sleep in garages and closets. Health care, if available, is tenuous, exacerbating illness and cutting lives short. Neighborhood schools offer only the minimum to students most in need of quality education. Children grow up barraged by messages that mock their heritage and brand them as enemy invaders and carriers of infestation. These are realities faced by the staff, children, families, and artists at Los Cenzontles.

To understand the deepest impact of Los Cenzontles' cultural work requires an understanding of the corrosive and insidious impact of shame imposed upon working-class people whose families immigrated from poor countries. Society stigmatizes poverty and otherness, teaching us to despise the poor and the marginalized, which then breeds shame. Despite the fact that deviant behavior exists in all social classes, only the poor are defined by it. Although poverty is an economic condition, not a personal defect, it is nevertheless treated as the latter, and this class stigma is further reinforced in literature, television, and film, impacting how we see ourselves and others. Shame has us deny our family stories and contributions, robbing our children of the guidance and nourishment of their elders, and rendering us invisible even to ourselves. When children of working-class immigrants willfully ignore the sacrifices of their parents, they are depriving themselves of their own ancestral resilience as well as the renewing power of gratitude.

It is painful to think of the centuries-old social pressures that are inflicted on people of color—pressures aimed at making us ashamed of our natures. We are led to believe that denying the curl of our hair, the color of our skin, and our facial features could render us acceptable to a bigoted society; as if denying our ancestral languages could possibly reassure those intolerant of the sounds we make; as if disguising our cultures—born of peoples enduring poverty and oppression—with the trappings of the rich could improve our condition. But denying our natures, our cultures, our histories does not bring acceptance. Only acceptance does.

In our 2008 documentary *Vivir*, Fabiola Trujillo's older brother Marin, commenting on our film *Pasajero, A Journey of Time and Memory*, says, "I think the way that Los Cenzontles has promoted culture has been very daring, courageous, and I think often misunderstood. And I say this as the brother of someone who is in Los Cenzontles. It wasn't until I saw the documentary that I got it, that I understood what you were try-ing to do, which was to bring the culture that has always been there, and to put it in front of us and say, 'We're also this,' and 'We were this,' and 'This is beautiful.'"

●●●

Hugo Arroyo backstage, 2011. Photo by Mike Melnyk

When, in the 2000s, we were being invited more and more often to perform on prestigious concert stages, I always felt a sense of accomplishment when Mexican immigrant service staff would come out of the kitchen to listen to us. Our 2001 Cuatro Maestros tour of California may have been the first in which our traditions were represented on major stages by artists who were primarily focused on family and community culture. Within a few years, touring grants allowed us to begin giving theatrical concerts at performing arts centers in communities across the country where Mexican migrants had settled, including North Carolina, Illinois, Georgia, Utah, Idaho, and Missouri. Our shows typically featured four regional styles of music and dance, all fully costumed and staged, and they were sometimes accompanied by workshops and screenings of our films, both efforts intended to help forge relationships between new and existing community members in those areas. After one show in Boise, Idaho, a young Latino audience member who was in the armed forces confided to me that our concert had made him feel proud of his heritage for the first time in his life.

I wrote my song "Valor Latino" as an anthem for acceptance, as well as a challenge. *Valor* means both "value" and "courage" in Spanish, and the song proclaims our value in this, our country, and encourages us to assume our rightful place within it. I have witnessed many social campaigns to promote ethnic pride that is predicated on a gentrified self-image, as if we need to be highly educated or financially successful to merit visibility. In this song, it was important for me to celebrate the breadth of our contributions. No job is unimportant.

VALOR LATINO

Tenemos la fama de raza obrera
Por eso de orgullo cantamos afuera
Construimos viviendas, calles y puentes
Sembramos cosechas que alimenta a la gente

Cuidamos a niños, enfermos y ancianos
Hacemos labores usando las manos
Tenemos negocios, somos empresarios
Jugamos deportes en grandes estadios

Amplifica tu voz (Valor Latino)
Escucha tu voz (Valor Latino)
Conoce tu voz (Valor Latino)
Respeta tu voz (Valor Latino)

Somos científicos, somos meseros
Somos pintores y somos vaqueros
Dentistas, doctores, poetas, soldados
Somos sacerdotes con rezos sagrados

Somos políticos y jardineros
Somos maestros y somos bomberos
Somos alumnos y amas de casa
Nos llaman latinos, hispanos y raza

Amplifica tu voz (Valor Latino)
Escucha tu voz (Valor Latino)
Conoce tu voz (Valor Latino)
Respeta tu voz (Valor Latino)

De nuestra cultura a nuestros valores
De nuestras canciones a nuestros sabores
De nuestra historia a nuestras creencias
De nuestro trabajo a nuestra paciencia

Con todo lo dicho con fuerza vayamos
Invierte lo bueno para superarnos
Cultiva las flores de nuestra raíz
Somos el futuro de nuestro país

Amplifica tu voz (Valor Latino)
Escucha tu voz (Valor Latino)
Conoce tu voz (Valor Latino)
Respeta tu voz (Valor Latino)

VALOR LATINO

We are known as working people
Which is why I sing out with pride
We build homes, streets, and bridges
We grow crops that feed people

We care for children, the sick, and the elderly
We work with our hands
We have businesses, we are entrepreneurs
We play sports in huge stadiums

Amplify your voice (Valor Latino)
Listen to your voice (Valor Latino)
Know your voice (Valor Latino)
Respect your voice (Valor Latino)

We are scientists, we are waiters
We are painters, and we are cowboys
Dentists, doctors, poets, and soldiers
We are priests with sacred prayers

We are politicians and gardeners
We are teachers and firefighters
We are students and housewives
We call ourselves Latinos, Hispanos, and Raza

Amplify your voice (Valor Latino)
Listen to your voice (Valor Latino)
Know your voice (Valor Latino)
Respect your voice (Valor Latino)

From our culture to our values
From our songs to our flavors
From our history to our beliefs
From our labor to our patience

With all that's been said, let's walk forward with strength
Invest in our good to rise up
Cultivate the flowers of our roots
We are the future of our country

Amplify your voice (Valor Latino)
Listen to your voice (Valor Latino)
Know your voice (Valor Latino)
Respect your voice (Valor Latino)

●●●

Throughout Los Cenzontles' three-decade history, politicians have regularly stirred up the anti-immigrant sentiments that are always simmering below society's surface. In 1994, California's Proposition 187 targeted undocumented laborers, some of the state's most productive and vulnerable people, blatantly ignoring the role the US played in creating the conditions that made migration a necessity. Under this scheme immigrants were being invited here and provided work with a wink and a nod by US companies that routinely sent trucks to the border to bring workers to factories and slaughterhouses around the country. American families also knowingly hire undocumented people to work in their homes and gardens, even as they accuse immigrants of stealing jobs. But they are stealing nothing. To the contrary, the US economy and American consumers benefit enormously from this system, but it is only the workers who, while bearing no responsibility for global economic policies, are branded as illegal and punished. I believe that societies have the right to enforce norms, laws, and borders, but if we really want to curtail the system of undocumented labor, then we must punish the corporations, businesses, and individuals who benefit from it, which includes allowing consumers to suffer the economic consequences.

Unfortunately, scapegoating Mexicans and Mexican Americans remains politically tenable because American culture has successfully branded us as illegitimate. And this targeting of "illegal aliens" affects not only undocumented people but *all* Latinos, especially the dark-skinned. Just a few years ago, a middle-aged white neighbor of mine, emboldened by opportunistic politicians and media outlets like Fox News, drunkenly assaulted me in front of my house, calling me an "illegal." The police refused to press charges against the man until I pressured the district attorney. I can attest from a lifetime of experience that anti-Latino discrimination is usually not taken seriously unless we go to extraordinary measures to demand it.

After Arizona enacted its Senate Bill 1070 anti-immigrant legislation in 2010, I composed a song called "Arizona, Estado de Vergüenza" (Arizona, State of Shame) as a real-time contribution to the mass protests across the country. I recorded myself singing it and made a simple video with its text. A few months later, we recorded a new version with Fabiola and Lucina singing, accompanied on string instruments by Hugo Arroyo, Emiliano, and me. The song was produced by Ry Cooder in Southern California, and it was made into a music video by legendary documentary filmmaker Les Blank. I have heard that the song was indeed played at protests.

ARIZONA, ESTADO DE VERGÜENZA

Este corrido canto yo con mucha pena
De la desgracia que ocurrió en la nación
Esta ley que han pasado en Arizona
Que legaliza la discriminación

Por falta del valor moral y fortaleza
La inmigración se niega a reformar
Ahora sufrirá la gente que trabaja
Y las familias separadas seguirán

Arizona, estado de vergüenza
¿Qué has hecho con tu miedo y tu temor?
En vez de ser famoso por tu hermosura
Tú tienes fama de racismo y rencor

¿Ahora gente, cómo vamos a seguir?
Esta ignorancia destruirá la sociedad.
¿O continuamos espantados y callados?
¿O decidimos que por fin hay que gritar?

Ya es tiempo de pararse con mucho orgullo
Por el valor que traemos a la nación
Con nuestras voces, votos y nuestro dinero
No permitamos ya la discriminación

Arizona, estado de vergüenza
¿Qué has hecho con tu miedo y tu temor?
En vez de ser famoso por tu hermosura
Tú tienes fama de racismo y rencor

ARIZONA, STATE OF SHAME

I sing this ballad with great pain
About a disgrace that is happening in our country
They passed a law in Arizona
That legalizes discrimination

For a lack of moral strength and fortitude
They refuse to reform immigration laws
And now working people suffer
And families will continue to separate

Arizona, state of shame,
What have you done with your fear?
Instead of being known for your beauty
You are now famous for racism and hatred

Now people, how do we go forward?
This ignorance will destroy our society.
Do we continue to be scared and mute?
Or do we decide at last to scream out?

It is time to stand with pride
For the value we bring to the nation
With our voices, votes, and our money
We will not permit any more discrimination

Arizona, state of shame,
What have you done with your fear?
Instead of being known for your beauty
You are now famous for racism and hatred

I see politics as a function of culture, not the other way around. And I think of folk culture as a public space where people of different backgrounds and ideologies can share thoughts and sentiments through art. If we can affect changes in social consciousness, we can find political solutions that are more lasting because they are grounded in culture.

Though songs with political messages have long been part of the folk tradition, I have normally tried to avoid political stridency, believing that teaching our students skills to express themselves is our greatest power. Confusing cultural identity with political propaganda reduces us, our histories, and our stories. At our academy, we do not indoctrinate children with political ideologies, as do some youth programs. Our job is to provide young people tools and space to think and do for themselves, not tell them what to think; they will make their own conclusions. Edgar Ramirez, one of our students in 1994, told me recently that being in Los Cenzontles as a fifteen-year-old was his way to say "fuck you" to racist sentiments. A Mexican American friend once told me that while he doesn't go much for "Latino pride," our work makes him proud.

By 2012, I had become fed up with America's culture wars, which I see as a struggle between the left and right political ideologies of the Northern Hemisphere, ideologies that have long used people and countries of color—mostly from the global South—as sidekicks and pawns, viewed only through their relationship to white men. When people of color are acknowledged, it's usually to showcase either white men's dominance or their benevolence—both sides of the same coin that relegates our existence to the margins. Whether in local, national, or international politics, I have seen our interests manipulated to serve the agendas of others while we are told to wait our turn or are demonized as being the "wrong kind of Latino." I wrote the song "La Pelota" (The Ball) as a commentary about Latino voters being wooed before elections but then ignored afterward. Our companion music video, which features a cameo by Mexican rock star Saúl Hernández, advocates for Latinos to use their purchasing and voting power to promote our own varied interests.

LA PELOTA	THE BALL
Pobrecita la pelota	Poor ball
Ganas me dan de llorar	It makes me want to cry
La razón de que te agotas	The reason you're so tired
Es que no dejan de patear	Is that they don't stop kicking you
Te dicen que te quieren	They say they love you
Antes de la jugada	Before the game
Pero en vez de darte un beso	But instead of a kiss
Te da otra patada	They give you the boot
Ay, pelota	Oh, ball
Me gusta la pelota	I like the ball
Ay, pelota	Oh, ball
Pateando la pelota	Kicking the ball
Ay, pelota	Oh, ball
Queremos la pelota	We love the ball
Ay, pelota	Oh, ball
Pateando la pelota	Kicking the ball
Pateada por la izquierda	Kicked from the left
Pateada por la derecha	Kicked from the right
Después de que te usan	After they use you
A un lado te desechan	They throw you to the side
Pateada por arriba	Kicked from above
Pateada por abajo	Kicked from below
Y nadie escucha	And no one listens
Tus quejas. ¡Ay carajo!	To your complaints, oh damn!

Ay, pelota	Oh, ball
Me gusta la pelota	I like the ball
Ay, pelota	Oh, ball
Pateando la pelota	Kicking the ball
Ay, pelota	Oh, ball
Queremos la pelota	We love the ball
Ay, pelota	Oh, ball
Pateando la pelota	Kicking the ball

I also wrote the song "No Politics" in 2012 about what we miss in life because of our fixation on culture wars. Its message and infectious rhythm never failed to animate audiences, and reactions to the song made it clear that I was not the only one who was tired of the hyper-partisan state of our country. However, during the presidential election of 2016, I lost the heart to perform the song, as politics had taken a deadly, and deeply personal, turn. The fight was no longer ideological but existential to the fate of our representational democracy, which is our best chance to advance our country's promise of equality.

Also in 2012, Linda Ronstadt introduced us to Jackson Browne, a powerhouse in the music industry, whose music I had adored as a young person. When I was ten years old, my aunt Marie, my father's youngest sister, who was a generational bridge for us, took me to hear him at the Hollywood Bowl. It was my very first concert, and I have been a fan of his ever since. Jackson has always had an affinity for Mexican Americans, with whom he grew up in the Highland Park neighborhood of Los Angeles. As a teen seeking connections between my Mexican and American selves, his songs with Mexican overtones, like "Linda Paloma" and "Our Lady of the Well," especially resonated with me.

Linda thought that Jackson and David Hidalgo would sing well together and suggested they harmonize on my song "The Silence," which I had composed about the horrific drug

violence in Mexico. When I was working on its lyrics, I asked
writer Richard Rodriguez—whose reflections about Mexican
American identity helped shape my own—for clues on how to
address such a vast and tragic subject. He suggested that I scour
the poems of Emily Dickinson to find a template, which I did in
her poem "Glee! The great storm is over!" Modeling songs after
existing songs and poems is as old as songwriting itself.

At the time, Dave was coproducing our *Regeneration* album
and we were scheduled to record overdubs in Los Angeles.
Jackson introduced us to a studio in Echo Park and joined us.
And of course, Linda was correct: David's and Jackson's voices
resonated with each other beautifully.

THE SILENCE

Dance when the storm is over
Sing when torment's passed
Sigh when fists of tortured death
Release this arid land

Mourn the tens of thousands
Pray for the grieving shell
Bless the cursed noble womb
That bore this muted hell

How do we spin this tale
Tongues freed from fear at last
Answers to our children when
They ask us what has passed?

When silence breaks from telling
And finally we can cry
What will we reveal then
When they ask us why?

At that session, Jackson told us of a song that he had begun some years before but was never able to finish. He, David, and I began to work on it at the studio. His original verses read: "The Klan is down on the border / They say they want law and order." He updated them to "The Minutemen are on the border . . . ," but I asked him if we could write about us instead of them. I proposed: "Just a child when she crossed the border / To reunite with her father." That was the beginning of "The Dreamer," a song loosely based on Lucina's story of coming to this country as an undocumented eleven-year-old.

THE DREAMER

Just a child when she crossed the border
To reunite with her father
Who had traveled north to support her
So many years before

She left half her family behind her
And with a crucifix to remind her
She pledged her future to this land
And does the best that she can do

¿A dónde van los sueños
Nacidos de la fe y la ilusión
Donde no hay camino ni huella
Solo deseos que susurran al corazón?

Eagles fly on columns of the wind
    Viviendo en el viento (Living on the wind)
Fish swim the currents of the sea
    Qué libre el mar (How free the sea)
People cross oceans and deserts and rivers
    Cruzamos el río (We crossed the river)

Carrying nothing more than the dream
of what life could be

Today she got the order
They're taking steps to deport her
To send her back over the border
And tear her away from the life she has made

We don't see half the people around us
But we imagine enemies who surround us
And the walls that we've built between us
Keep us prisoners of our fears

¿A dónde van los sueños
    Where do the dreams go
Nacidos de la fe y la ilusión
    Born of faith and illusion
Donde no hay camino ni huella
    Where there's no road and no footprints
Solo deseos que susurran al corazón?
    Only desires that whisper to the heart?

We later recorded "The Dreamer" with Jackson at his studio and he released it as a single along with a video shot at Los Cenzontles and created by celebrated music video director Mark Kohr. Jackson then recorded another version with his band for his 2021 album *Downhill from Everywhere*, which was a thrill to hear. As I age, I encounter more and more moments in which my life seems to come full circle. Such was hearing Jackson sing "The Dreamer" live in concert at Berkeley's Greek Theater, giving a shout-out to me, Lucina, and Los Cenzontles.

In 2014, we produced a short animated video called *Tata's Gift* with another grant from the Creative Work Fund. Designed

Lucina performing with Jackson Browne, 2013. Photo by Craig Sherod

and animated by filmmaker Dionisio Ceballos, it tells the story, with images and original music, of a boy who is being bullied but finds strength within a video game dream in which his departed Tata, or grandfather, appears with cultural gifts that help the boy defeat his foe. Students, family members, and friends of Los Cenzontles play the animated characters; Marie-Astrid created the folk art used in the dream sequence with Huichol yarn-painting techniques; and Lucina and I wrote songs in English and in Spanish. When we screen the film for schoolchildren, they respond with great emotion to the bonding scenes between the boy and his grandparents. I myself still sometimes tear up when the boy embraces his grandmother, thinking of my own.

Bearing the brunt of society's shame takes a toll. For me, even simple, sincere declarations of pride can make me feel emotional. A journalist friend who is not Mexican but has written brilliantly about Mexican society once mocked our song "The Dreamer" as having a naive "up with la gente" message. But we had composed the song with sincerity about someone we know, and to us the message was as authentic as the emotions that had inspired it. My friend's casual cynicism reminded me that even a person who understands many aspects of our culture may still be unable to feel what it is like to be us. I once asked a veteran Chicano musician about how he and his bandmates managed to put up with years of anti-Mexican bias. He replied with dry Chicano humor, "Why do you think we drink so much?"

I wrote my song "Free to Be Me" in 2012 as a lighthearted jab at living with stereotypes, but its underlying message cuts to the heart of how I have lived my life and done my work. Its final verse could be my epitaph.

FREE TO BE ME

We come from California
We make it understood
So we're just a little puzzled when they tell us
You speak English real good

And when Emiliano
With such a noble name
Tells 'em that he doesn't speak Espanish
They think it's really such a shame

I just wanna be free to be me

When our shows are over
I'd love to stay out later
But when I walk by, people hand me their basura
Because they think that I'm the waiter

And others recognize us
And say, "Hey, let's go and hang"
But get so disappointed when they find out
That we were never in a gang

I just wanna be free to be me

Fabiola and Lucina
Are really good in la cocina
They make ceviche, enchiladas, chilaquiles,
But they take out comida china

And this here is Mireya
She grew up in San Pablo
She can dance hip-hop and la quebradita
And she can do the zapateado

I just wanna be free to be me

Now here's my simple message
And it's no paradox
No matter if they're strangers or familia
Don't let them put you in a box

So listen, chavalitos
Who are living in dos mundos
Just roll it up and put it all together
There's really nothing mas profundo

Emiliano Rodriguez backstage, 2011. Photo by Mike Melnyk

CHAPTER 15

●●●

LINDA RONSTADT

When I met Linda Ronstadt in 1993, her *Canciones de Mi Padre* (1987) and *Mas Canciones* (1991) mariachi albums were reverberating through the streets of San Pablo and Richmond. Almost every Mexican girl in the neighborhood, few of whom knew her English-language hits "You're No Good" and "It's So Easy," imitated her version of the classic ranchera "Los Laureles" . . . or tried to. Meeting Linda not only made Los Cenzontles' 1993 trip to Veracruz possible, it marked the beginning of a long friendship that has enriched the trajectory of our work.

Linda concerns herself not only with music but with issues of humanity, sustainability, and the well-being of children. She has always been gracious with us, but earning her trust was not immediate, and it has been only in the last few years that I have allowed myself to be silly with her. I can't imagine the kind of pressures that someone of her celebrity must contend with, and

I always want to be considerate of that, but eventually I figured that even celebrities need friends, and I wanted to be among hers. Of course, every once in a while I am reminded of her incredible accomplishments and I again become just another awkward fan.

Linda often claims that she doesn't like to listen to her old recordings. Journalists usually characterize this as self-effacement, but I think it would be more accurate to say that she is matter-of-fact by nature, and she has immense respect for music. So, when she listens to her singing from the past, she hears—now with the benefit of her accumulated wisdom—what she would *want* it to be, in service of the song. When she made her Mexican albums, she took every aspect seriously. She worked hard to learn to sing rancheras and huapangos with authenticity, and she did so with both refinement and guts, something that I consider the highest goal in interpreting traditional music. There are plenty of gutsy musicians without refinement, and there are refined musicians who play without guts, but both miss the mark. Linda nailed it. Mariachis that play kitsch, of which there are many, annoy me the most. Her *Canciones* recordings, in contrast, were performed, arranged, and produced with impeccable taste and artistry, and they have had a profound impact on Latinos precisely because of the painstaking care and attention that she breathed into them.

Though I have never collaborated with Linda on a full professional music project, I feel that we have collaborated in many other ways. And she has certainly been a generous advisor to me. I once asked her what she thought about Los Cenzontles working with a particular popular musician. She replied that all musical decisions must be based on music and not on celebrity, teaching me that if we lose sight of the integrity of the music, we risk diminishing its holistic power—advice that applies to other aspects of our work as well. Whenever I am faced with an opportunity that deviates from our core mission, I think of her and remain steady.

Linda has introduced us to many wonderful people, and she has attended, and hosted, numerous meetings to help Los Cenzontles attract support. It was because of her, for example, that comedian Cheech Marin played *Celebrity Jeopardy!* on our behalf in 1998. (Each celebrity player donates their winnings to a charity of choice.) I believe that her long support of our program has confused some people, though. One might expect her, as one of the great voices of the twentieth century, to support an exclusive school for the highly gifted. And that is not who we are. Our organization is not based on the talent of any individual but on the manner in which we work together. In fact, "talent" is a word I prefer to avoid when discussing youth arts education, because it can hinder those both with and without it. Such branding can discourage late bloomers, while pressuring prodigies to perform prematurely for the wrong reasons. What matters most in music is whether we have something to communicate, and that takes time to figure out. Linda, who has likened our approach to the Slow Food movement, which promotes honoring traditions and local sources, learned music in her home, where she was exposed to an exceptionally broad repertory at an early age. She understands the benefits of children learning music in a family-like setting, such as Los Cenzontles Academy, and feels that we should not relegate singing to just professionals. In other words, we share core values.

Linda has also been a fierce defender. A few years ago I was interviewed by a representative of a local foundation that was considering our grant proposal. During our phone call, the woman complained that Mexicans had ruined their local school district because they don't value education, and that Mexican men mistreated their wives and neglected their families. She then warned me that if her foundation gave us money, we must not use it to write songs about drug traffickers. We did not receive the grant, and no one at the foundation responded to my letter of protest about the call. I might have just filed this episode away with other such incidents, except that one day Linda asked me if we received support from that foundation, which had asked her to perform at their fundraiser. So, I told her my story. Within a week, she had scheduled a lunch meeting with me, her, and the foundation's executive director, who apologized to me more than a few times. They then began to support our work.

While recording our 2008 album *Songs of Wood & Steel* with David Hidalgo, we invited Linda to sing a duet with him. We didn't have a song that took full advantage of her vocal abilities, but she agreed to sing "El Chubasco," a popular ranchera composed by Antonio Aguilar and for which we had created a humble arrangement. Recording Linda and David at our storefront studio was both thrilling and daunting. Of course, both were gracious, and their voices filled our space with warmth and color. Later, Dave confided that he teared up while listening to the track; its sincerity, he said, made it sound as if it were being sung by siblings.

That same year, we met Linda backstage at the Hardly Strictly Bluegrass festival, an outdoor, multistage event in San Francisco's Golden Gate Park. By her side, Marie-Astrid, Emiliano, Lucina, Fabiola, and I hung out with David Hidalgo, Chris Strachwitz of Arhoolie Records, Linda's longtime friend Emmylou Harris, and Warren Hellman, the philanthropist whose generosity made the free annual event possible and whose family continues to support our work. We then went to listen to Los Lobos from the side of the stage, after which Linda asked if we could give her a ride home. I cautioned her that our car was already at seatbelt capacity, but she said she didn't need a seatbelt, and so we all climbed into my car. I thought about stories of Linda catching rides with friends in Los Angeles in the early 1970s, but this time it was not through Laurel Canyon but San Francisco's Richmond District.

Linda is versed in many subjects beyond music, and she is just as generous with her knowledge and talents in those areas.

When we expanded our storefront to add a kitchen, she accompanied us to the design store to help us choose materials, and when we built our new art room, which Marie-Astrid oversees, she weighed in on some of the architectural details. When the contractor resisted the idea of cutting windows into the cinderblock exterior wall—something Marie-Astrid wanted because it would provide much-needed natural light—Linda told me, "If you love your wife, you will insist on those windows." I conveyed her sense of urgency to the contractor, and it was done. The art room is now a beautifully lit, colorful space for our students to explore their abilities in creating folk arts and jewelry. It is the sparkling eyes of our academy, just as the production studio is its ears. The hardwood floor where students dance is its lungs. And the kitchen is its heart.

Marie-Astrid and Linda Ronstadt at Los Cenzontles' fashion show, 2011. Photo by Mike Melnyk

Over the years, Linda has visited our academy many times to accompany our children in their singing, dance, and art classes. After one such visit around Thanksgiving 2018, she invited us to perform in Banámichi, Sonora, where her grandfather Federico had been born and raised. Linda had mentioned traveling there before, but this was an actual plan for February 2019, giving us eight weeks to prepare and raise travel funds, an exciting opportunity but a daunting task, especially given that the work needed to happen over the Christmas and New Year break. The parents of seventeen Los Cenzontles students ages eight and up quickly agreed to allow us to take their children on the trip. Marie-Astrid spent nearly every waking hour of the holidays crocheting newly designed blouses for our female performers, and Emiliano readied our instruments and purchased custom flight cases for what was the largest group of musicians we had ever traveled with. Lucina and Fabiola prepared the children for a show that we had never performed.

Out of respect for her privacy, and not wanting to exploit our friendship, I rarely asked Linda for photos or videos when we met with her, but on this occasion, recognizing the rare opportunity of this historic trip, I asked her if we could film the adventure, and she agreed without hesitation. I contracted filmmaker Armando Aparicio, whom I had met through James Hall, to assemble a crew while I worked on concepts that were based on a keynote address that we gave for the 2011 Grantmakers in the Arts conference. The conference theme that year was "Embracing the Velocity of Change." In our presentation, Linda and I took turns telling stories of family and the impact of music. Our narratives were interwoven with performances by Los Cenzontles with David Hidalgo. Although we received a sustained standing ovation from the audience, made up of people from powerful foundations from across the nation, we did not raise a single dollar, demonstrating that the velocity of change in philanthropy is actually quite slow.

In 2002, the year that we lost all California Arts Council funding, I scrambled to find alternative income to sustain our work. Fortunately, the statewide James Irvine Foundation had just announced a new grant initiative to reach underserved California communities in response to demographic changes and the rise of digital technology. With their support, we began to produce documentary films as a way to reach and inspire other communities through storytelling. In the following five years, we produced our "Cultures of Mexico in California" documentary series, which included our films *Pasajero, A Journey of Time and Memory; Fandango, Searching for the White Monkey;* and *Vivir* (To Live), each of which captured different aspects of our work.

While trying to figure out how to begin creating our first film, *Pasajero,* I interviewed a producer with PBS experience. When he told me it would be unethical for us to produce a film about ourselves, not only did I sense that he was jockeying for the job but I began to understand why there are so few stories about communities like ours, and why the ones that did exist all felt the same, lacking in dimension. Biases in media and academia around third-person objectivity ensure that our stories are only told by outsiders, people who never fully get to know us and who repeat the same shallow stories of "discovery," which I call "Christopher Columbus syndrome." I knew that if we wanted to tell our stories with nuance and authenticity, we would have to fully partner with filmmakers and maintain final control. Further, to pave a way for others to tell their own stories, I also insisted that we be credited as cocreators of the films. Since that time, we have produced twenty films, hundreds of music videos, and more than thirty musical albums recognized for their first-voice authenticity. A veteran filmmaker recently remarked about my ability to continue to find stories within our community after so many years. I replied that there is no shortage of stories when we look closely at the people around us as they adapt to ever-changing circumstances.

One morning in December 2018, while we were getting ready to perform "The Dreamer" with Jackson Browne at a San

Francisco human rights event, Linda called me. I cheerily told her that we were with Jackson, and she immediately replied, "Invite him to Mexico!" I turned to Jackson and said, "Do you want to come to Mexico with Linda and us?" He quickly replied, "Of course!" I've always known that Linda was a mastermind. It was she, after all, who had assembled the backup band that would become the Eagles. And only she could have managed to get three top mariachis—who were fierce competitors with each other!—to cooperate on her *Canciones* projects. Even after she could no longer sing, she has continued to put people together to advance projects that are important to her.

This trip to Banámichi would include members of Linda's family, her friends, and people for whom she had prospective projects in mind. One of her projects was to introduce our children to a group of young folklórico dancers in Sonora that she also supported. Another was a cookbook that morphed into her memoir *Feels Like Home: A Song for the Sonoran Borderlands*, with writer Lawrence Downes and photographer Bill Steen. And yet another was to be in a place that made her happy and with people she cared for. When I told Ry Cooder about the trip, he simply replied, "Linda does things right." At the beginning of the new year, four weeks before our trip to Sonora, we secured sponsorship for our travel expenses from San Francisco philanthropist Nion McEvoy, and with that all of the pieces were in place.

About five weeks before the trip, Linda asked me if I wanted director James Keach to come along to direct our film and pay for its production. He was producing a documentary about her career for CNN called *Linda Ronstadt: The Sound of My Voice*, for which she had not yet granted an onscreen interview. She told him that she would do one in Mexico if he also made our film. As she had done so many times before, Linda was leveraging her influence on our behalf.

While I understood the value of having a man of Keach's talent, resources, and connections making our film, I also saw the risks of getting sidelined by a Hollywood producer. Linda had always been fair with us, and never condescending, but the same cannot be said of some other powerful people, who have been known to treat us dismissively, or worse. After careful consideration, I decided to accept the offer, with the condition that the collaboration be a business agreement and not a favor. After all, we were not entering into the situation empty-handed. We had a theme, a cast, the music, travel funds, a production crew, and Linda's agreement to participate. So, our entertainment attorney, MJ "Bo" Bogatin, drafted a contract that stipulated that Keach's company and Los Cenzontles would share mutual responsibility for creative content and that we would receive coproduction credit. Keach hired Armando's crew and agreed to our conditions just hours before the trip. If he had not, we were fully prepared to go without him.

Early on Valentine's Day 2019, a yellow school bus took our group of twenty-one Cenzontles to the San Jose International Airport, which had the only direct flight from the Bay Area to Tucson. The children's mothers made us breakfast burritos for the ride, and the kids all wore new light-blue hoodies printed with the Los Cenzontles logo to make it easier for the adults to keep track of them along the route. As we had never traveled with such a large group of children, I nervously counted and recounted blue hoodies at the airport, and then we were off to Arizona.

The day before our trip, a national border emergency was declared by the president—not because there was an actual emergency but to provoke white fear of Mexican migrants. After spending the night in a hotel in Nogales, Arizona, we got up early to meet the film crew, who was arriving before Linda's bus, to shoot an interview with Lucina about her undocumented border crossing. It would be the first time she would speak about her experience publicly, but she had hesitantly agreed to do it because of her commitment to this Los Cenzontles project and with the understanding that her story could help others process and express their experiences of trauma. The interview was set up under a newly installed barbed wire fence, and as Lucina wept on camera, recalling the fear and shame that never fully disappears, a Border Patrol car passed behind her, making the moment that much more poignant and menacing.

When Linda's bus rolled in from Tucson with Jackson and Linda's friends and family members, we jumped on board and all headed toward Sonora, Mexico. Our path through the Sonoran Desert had been traveled for thousands of years by Native people and was the route for the Anza expedition, which, in 1776, established a Spanish outpost in what would become San Francisco. Later in 2019, the National Park Service commissioned us to compose a corrido and companion music video about that journey, to raise awareness of historical Latino contributions to our land. The history of mankind, after all, is replete with stories of migration. But of course the border that we were now crossing looked nothing like it had in Linda's youth, when people passed easily back and forth. What we saw was a militarized zone, appearing like an oozing sore on ancient land, obstructing both history and nature.

As we traveled south, the desert continued to reveal its beauty. We stopped to have lunch in the backyard of a humble home in the small rural village of Cucurpe. Members of Los Cenzontles first played and danced, and then Linda's cousin Bobby and nephew Peter sang and played guitar and accordion. During one song, I heard the breathtaking sound of Linda's voice. She was seated next to me, quietly singing a third harmony, and I wished that the rest of the world could hear her as well.

Our bus continued on increasingly twisting roads and rolling hills toward the Sonora River Valley. When Linda and

Jackson toured by bus in the 1970s, they were surrounded by rock 'n' roll musicians, some of whom invariably had hangovers. This one was filled with children playing Mexican folk music. Jackson, who sometimes joined in on his travel ukulele, was a kindred spirit throughout the trip, helping at every turn. I recently saw him in concert and marveled at the way he held the audience's attention for nearly three hours, his voice only made richer by time. Yet, on our trip, he was one of us, coiling microphone cables, hanging out with the kids and guests, and providing invaluable advice on issues of sound and shooting locations.

Finally, we arrived at Banámichi, a picturesque but relatively empty pueblo that had last seen greater economic prosperity in the distant past. We settled into our bed-and-breakfast and then set out to enjoy the town's tranquility, local food, bacanora liquor, and the company around us. The children had time to play freely in town and eat Sonoran hot dogs, churros, and the delicious large flour tortillas that are a specialty of the region. One evening after dinner, Jackson sang in the small dining room for our group of travelers, all of whom were adoring fans. Among the songs he played was "Our Lady of the Well," which he had written about Mexico years before having visited it. Together, Jackson, Lucina, and Fabiola sang "Deportee (Plane Wreck at Los Gatos)," whose lyrics were written by Woody Guthrie after a tragic incident in 1948, underscoring the fact that inhumane treatment of Mexican migrants is nothing new.

Word began circulating that Linda had agreed to be filmed singing with Bobby and Peter for the CNN film. They would sing the song I had heard at lunch in Cucurpe: "A la Orilla de un Palmar," a lovely Mexican canción from the mid-nineteenth century that has been sung in the Ronstadt family for generations. The performance was filmed in the large living room of a historic home while the rest of us waited on the other side of a closed door. When Linda emerged from the room, we all greeted her enthusiastically. She simply said to us, "I'm hungry. What's for dinner?" When it was my turn to give her a hug, she whispered to me, "I'm glad we are friends."

Our visit to Banámichi lasted only three days, every minute of which was filled with work for Los Cenzontles' adults. Lucina and Fabiola cared for the children while also preparing them for the performance. Neither has chosen to have her own children, but they have both nurtured hundreds throughout the years. Marie-Astrid was also at work meticulously ironing and steaming two different costumes for each performer, while Emiliano set up and tuned our twenty-some instruments, and I planned the shows and the film production and gave interviews that framed the film's themes. Los Cenzontles performed two shows, each with three regional Mexican styles of music and dance, on two consecutive days in the plazas of Banámichi and nearby Arizpe, where expedition leader Juan Bautista de Anza is buried. Our performances were received warmly by locals and visitors, and I felt proud, and relieved.

Oswaldo and Natalie dance "El Torero" (The Bullfighter) in Banámichi, Sonora, 2019. Photo by Bill Steen

Our trip back to Arizona was magical. Without the film crew, which Keach had pulled out early after having captured Linda's shots for the CNN film, we stopped for a quiet lunch of sopa de queso and tamales on the lush banks of the Río Sonora. Linda, Jackson, Los Cenzontles, and family and friends quietly reflected on the days we had spent together and, more generally, on the journey of life. At the conclusion of this intensely rich and purposeful trip, the whisper of the breeze as the children gently explored the river reminded me of life's impermanence. Before long, we reboarded the bus and headed back home.

Six months later, in August 2019, we resumed shooting our film in San Pablo. Days before, an assassin spurred on by the president's racist calls to action, had just massacred twenty-three Mexicans and Mexican Americans at a Walmart in El Paso, Texas. With emotions frayed, we interviewed the Cenzontles families of Juan and Tere Ortega and of Tomas Velazquez and Magda Resendiz, whose children had gone to Banámichi with us. During our interview at the home of the hardworking Velazquez-Resendiz family, seventeen-year-old Favio surprised us by recounting a powerful and tearful incident from his childhood about the time his father, a landscaper, was detained by ICE (US Immigration and Customs Enforcement). I learned later that, the night before the shoot, the family had discussed whether to tell the story at all. And though both parents had still not completely resolved their immigration status, they decided to go forward, even if it exposed them to some risk. The resulting scene revealed the deeper vulnerability, normally kept private, that many Mexican American families live with daily.

Linda and the Mockingbirds was released in 2020. It is a strong and moving film, in part because it was created with a shared vision, merging Hollywood production values and resources with first-voice access and authenticity. In an age when we increasingly recognize visibility as essential to our humanity, and cultural appropriation as a liability, I believe that mutual partnerships such as these are a model.

In March 2022, Linda visited our academy to enjoy an afternoon of music by Los Cenzontles and singer Marisol "La Marisoul" Hernandez and her group Son California. Together we played in the traditional style of the son jarocho, whose revival was boosted so many years ago by Linda's support of our 1993 trip to Veracruz. La Marisoul is among the finest heirs to our Mexican and Chicano lineages—ones that include Lola Beltrán, Lalo Guerrero, Los Lobos, and Linda Ronstadt. Her respect for our cultural history, tradition bearers, and next-generation artists adds the depth of time to her remarkable vocal prowess. She grew up on Olvera Street in Downtown Los Angeles, where her family runs a kiosk. She learned from the musicians who make their living playing in Olvera Street's bars and restaurants, and perhaps that is one of the reasons I feel connected to her, since when I was young my family regularly visited Olvera Street. In the 1920s, my grandmother Enriqueta Guillen bought masa at what was then a La Luz del Dia grocery store. My father and son were both baptized at Nuestra Señora la Reina de los Ángeles across the street. And I continued to eat French dip sandwiches with my father at the nearby Philippe The Original until his death in 2016.

One of my favorite scenes captured in our short film *Linda & La Marisoul: An Afternoon at Los Cenzontles* happened toward the end of our visit, when I asked Marisol to sit next to Linda and sing her a song, sola. With her jarana in hand, she sang "Todo Cambia" (Everything Changes), a powerfully reflective song made famous by Argentine singer Mercedes Sosa. Alongside the generations of musicians present, and reflecting on the passage of time, I could not help but cry while she sang. And I was not the only one. Many others in the room were holding back tears as well, including Marisol, who bravely continued to sing through her emotions. The clear-eyed Linda Ronstadt, a woman of steely determination who I have heard rarely cries, began to tear up as well. I feel profoundly privileged to have lived this remarkable moment, among so many others, just as I am privileged to have Linda in my life.

CHAPTER 16

●●●

SONGS FOR STRANGE TIMES

In early March 2020, as we became increasingly concerned about the COVID-19 pandemic, Marie-Astrid and her two fifteen-year-old jewelry students, Joeceline Garcia and Isabel Reyes, traveled to Yucatán to study embroidery in Mayan communities. I looked for ways to send a professional videographer to capture their journey, before realizing that it would unduly interfere with the intimacy of their experience. So, instead, I asked Marie-Astrid, who had filmed so many of our adventures throughout the years, to shoot their trip on her iPhone. Our filmmaker friend James Hall also gave the teens a brief training on the basics of shooting, lent them simple video cameras, and asked them to interview each other every evening.

The day after they returned, California declared a lockdown, a sudden closing of the world that rendered their colorful images of Mayan art and artisans, and their treasure trove of stories, that much more precious. Editing footage from their week in Yucatán served as profound consolation throughout those difficult months to come. To their images, James added Marie-Astrid's emotionally candid reflections and created our documentary *Puntos de Vida (Threads of Life)*, an achingly poignant film.

As the pandemic deepened, we grew increasingly anxious about how long it would last, and if we would survive. Indeed, some family members of our students died of the virus, as did many Bay Area Latino essential workers. But I knew that we had to find a way to not only seamlessly continue our work but expand it. We quickly transitioned to online classes and increased our instruction time to compensate for technical complications. We also canceled all class fees (which were already modest) to reduce financial stress on our families. I didn't know if we would be able to recover the lost revenue, but I never questioned that we had to do everything possible to serve our students. These are the moments that culture is meant to remedy. To do less would have been failing our community, our mission, and our values.

We have always adjusted our programming to meet the changing needs of our community, but never quite as urgently as during the COVID-19 pandemic. As the lockdown was repeatedly extended, our teachers—Ricardo Rosales, Silvestre Martinez, Sandy Poindexter, Marie-Astrid, Lucina, and Fabiola—patiently worked through the myriad glitches of Zoom with our children. Teaching jewelry online required that Marie-Astrid prepare each class by writing down every step of her intricate beading process and then delivering the handwritten instructions and supplies to each student's home in a brown paper sack the day before class, fully masked. It was an especially detailed exercise, but more than worthwhile. Her teen students, in kind, were even more attentive and appreciative during this time when the value of artistic engagement was acute. And the many benefits of those activities are still revealing themselves. For instance, in 2022, after their high school graduations, Isabel entered UC Davis to study film and animation, and Joeceline got a job repairing jewelry while attending college.

In every sense, the holistic structure of our organization was the key to our resilience. Our trusting relationships with our students and their families enabled us to quickly adapt to new ways of working. To replace live recitals, our children instead prepared to participate in media projects with our production partners. The first was a music video in May 2020, modeled after the Playing for Change series, in which musicians are captured separately in various parts of the world and then edited together. We filmed separate performances of "El Colas" with fifteen students, me, Fabiola, and Lucina in various outdoor spaces, as well as David Hidalgo outside his Southern California home. Everyone sang a verse or did an instrumental solo. It took a great deal of time and effort to prepare the kids, coordinate the arrangements and shoots, mix the music, and edit the video, but seeing everyone "together" onscreen brought wonderful, welcome relief to us all.

Because most of our students attend classes alongside their siblings, we organized them into family groups so they could practice at home. To follow up on "El Colas," I modeled a new video series after vintage ethnomusicology films that captured folk musicians playing in their natural environments. We visited the homes of five of our families to record and film, from a distance, our students performing at their front doors—a series that became our "Front Porch Sessions." A few months later, deeper into the pandemic, we created our more intimate "Backyard Sessions," in which we captured students playing and singing songs dedicated to someone they missed. All of these productions received ample media attention, including features on Bay Area television, an article in *Billboard* magazine, and broadcasts by the First Nations Experience network on PBS stations across the country.

Teaching online also enabled us to work with maestros outside of the country. Gilberto Gutiérrez began teaching workshops in traditional verse composition from his home in Veracruz to our students, notably Verenice Velazquez, who is cultivating a talent and passion for writing. Together they wrote verses that reflected on many aspects of life.

Me pongo a reflexionar	I begin to reflect
De estos años que han pasado	On these past few years
Y mucho daño han causado,	That have caused great pain,
Eso puedo asegurar.	That I can attest.
No nos deja descansar	We just cannot rest
Este vírus que nos pega.	From this virus that has hit us.
Pero la ocasión se llega	But now it is time
De tomar la decisión	To make a decision
De vivir con devoción,	To live with devotion,
Con pasión y con entrega.	With passion and dedication.

Despite the many challenges, none of our students dropped out in 2020. Our staff and faculty regularly met online to discuss the needs of each individual child, as well as how we were all coping. It was an emotional period, but one with an acute sense of purpose and connection.

The long-term impact of the pandemic on our youth is still not known. We observe that they are generally more socially awkward and self-conscious, traits that are exacerbated by our smartphone-centered culture. I worry that they are being robbed of the wonder of childhood, so essential to human learning and identity. But I am certain that their involvement in the arts has helped them remain open to themselves, their families, and their peers. Recently I asked a group of teens ages thirteen to fifteen why they had remained so dedicated to their study of music during this time. They replied, wearing masks partly because of COVID-19 concerns but also out of shyness, that they loved to listen to music and to play it. It soothed them. One said that it was her form of therapy.

I am very proud of the way we worked with our faculty, staff, and families to provide challenging and meaningful activities to our students. Together we created art and media projects that captured a historic moment in real time, providing consolation and inspiration to our community and beyond. I believe that such acts of cooperation, for the sake of our children, is culture at its best. It couldn't have contrasted more dramatically with the divisive chaos pushed by opportunistic politicians during this same period.

The year 2020 was made even more painful by ecological distress in Northern California. As wildfire smoke darkened Bay Area skies, there were many days in which we could not go outside to take walks, one of the few permitted activities that helped us cope with the pandemic. On top of that, the larger picture of unrest initiated by the police lynching of George Floyd provoked unusually urgent, candid, and nuanced conversations in philanthropic circles around social justice and inclusion. At the time, it felt like we might finally be able to address issues of discrimination that were formerly out of bounds, but, a few years out now, I suspect that these conversations will result mostly in just more new jargon and acronyms that give only the impression of change while actually reinforcing old biases and creating new hierarchies. In 2020 and 2021, foundations increased their giving levels in response to the pandemic, allowing us to breathe a sigh of relief, but by 2023, giving again dropped and we found ourselves facing our first budget deficit in over a decade.

Even before the pandemic, I was growing weary from the accumulated weight of responsibility and having to fight the same battles year after year. I used to believe that consistently doing groundbreaking and impactful work would help make our case easier, but I underestimated the stubborn power of bias, which has doomed many Latino arts organizations that have risen and fallen during my career. Maintaining our organization has required extraordinary tenacity, which takes a toll.

I think of the story of the policeman walking at night on a city street who encounters a man under a lamppost searching for his keys. "Where did you last have them?" asks the cop. "Over there," replies the man, pointing to a darkened alley, to which the cop responds, "Then why are you looking here?" The man replies, "Because the light here is better." People tend to seek solutions where it is convenient to look, rather than where they actually should be looking. And communities like ours are considered dark alleys.

●●●

When I was a child, I often felt disappointed by how adults dismissed and misunderstood children. I promised myself that when I grew up I wouldn't forget what it was like to be a child. Perhaps inevitably, I couldn't keep that promise. But I have tried my best, as only adults can do, to create a place for children to be children, and where their creativity can blossom. But protecting such a space from the world's corrosive forces is a heavy responsibility, and it can be difficult to balance being an adult protector with maintaining the open spirit required of a creative artist.

In a strange way, the tribulations of the pandemic shocked me into realigning my outlook by reminding me of the fragility of life, and by giving me the space to reflect on what is truly important. Twice in 2020, mating doves chose to build their nests on a planter on the porch of our home, just a few feet from the front door, revealing a timely truth: within gratitude exists sources of resilience. But it also became clearer that we needed to transition our organization even more toward team leadership. Los Cenzontles has always been a strong team, and the terms "staff" and "faculty" do not sufficiently capture the importance of the people at Los Cenzontles who embody our artistic trajectory, pedagogy, and voice. However, I have always borne the main burden of responsibility— something that would need to shift as we marched further into our fourth decade.

The isolation of the pandemic forced me to be more resourceful and to better manage my anxiety and the impatience that comes from it. Emiliano had moved out of our area to pursue his independence and his passion for film photography, and Marie-Astrid, with struggles of her own, spent most of her time quietly working on handicrafts. So, I found ways to keep myself busy with online work, preparing meals, and practicing music at home. I posted to social media many videos of myself playing music, not to create anything of lasting value but just to stay purposeful, and to avert melancholy. I drew upon whatever musical strengths I could muster and practiced them diligently. I did not have the steady groove of my son's bass playing to lean on, nor the voices of Fabiola and Lucina to weave around. It was just me, and I was not used to that. Most days, I thought of a song in English or Spanish that spoke to the moment, found a key that felt right, learned it, and played it as well as I could. You cannot predict when or how a creative notion strikes, but when it does, it opens up a space within your mind's eye and becomes a call that you feel compelled to follow. There are times when this feeling remains hidden for a long while, and other times when it cascades like a waterfall. It is a miracle that gives shape to time and space that would otherwise be mundane and empty.

About twelve years ago, I was diagnosed with severe sleep apnea. I stop breathing about fifty-five times an hour, a condition that deprives the body and mind of sleep in a manner that is akin to torture. It made my life, and the lives of those around me, miserable. Learning to use a CPAP machine, which opens my air passageways while I sleep, was a deeply frightening process that forced me to deal with lifelong issues I had in relation to breathing, which began, according to my mother, when I was born with the umbilical cord around my neck. That is why, perhaps, I avoided learning to sing for decades. But taking classes opened me up to many parts of myself that were previously frightening. Also, placing songs into my voice while simultaneously playing the guitar requires complex muscle coordination throughout the body and builds physical, mental, and emotional awareness, which is a thrilling journey of discovery.

When I was a young man, I had much within me that I needed to express, but it has taken me a lifetime to discover the refinements of that expression. Most of this I did not learn at school but from my experiences and the people around me. I try to express something within that both provides me personal moments of connection and will hopefully provoke a human response in others. At best, it might open a door for someone, somehow, somewhere. That is the crux of my career. And it has little to do with the world of professional music. It was my father's untrained voice, after all, that opened me up to the connective power of music. There is a place in the world for that.

In late 2021, I compiled some of the videos and photos I had posted on social media during the darkest times of the pandemic, threading them together to create a short video with filmmaker Mark Kohr called *Songs for Strange Times: 2020–21.* It turns out that many of my social media friends felt similarly isolated, and the music created a bond. As the pandemic becomes part of the past, this bond is something I hope never to forget.

The members of Los Cenzontles also continued to create music during that time. I am forever grateful to the musicians who recorded with us remotely. In addition to Fabiola and

Lucina, they included my former college bandmate the bassist Pablo Aslan, now a tango master living in New York City; master Cuban percussionist Carlos Caro, who lives in the San Joaquin Valley; Lev Zhurbin, a Russian string player and arranger in New York; Hector Espinoza; La Marisoul; David Hidalgo; and engineers David Luke and Greg Morgenstein. In all, we released twenty song singles during the depths of the pandemic lockdown. We later compiled them for our *Juntos a la Distancia* album, which we released in late 2021.

In April 2021, I suggested to Dave Hidalgo that we cover "Lo Siento Mi Vida," a song composed by Linda Ronstadt with her father, Gilbert Ronstadt, and her bandmate Kenny Edwards. I thought it would be cool to do a cover version with male voices, since most tributes to her are done by women. After all, I told Dave, "Linda likes guys," to which Dave instantly replied, "And guys like Linda." When considering a third musician to complete the three-part vocal harmony, he suggested Daniel Valdez, an old friend of Linda's and a Chicano legend whose performance in *Zoot Suit* at the Mark Taper Forum in 1978 was pivotal for me as a teen. I felt that recording "Lo Siento Mi Vida" with Daniel Valdez and David Hidalgo would be a tribute not only to Linda but to our Chicano cultural legacy—another moment in which my life would come full circle.

●◖●

My father died in September 2016. His health had been in a steep decline, and the loss of independence made him miserable. My brothers, Gregory and Phillip, who live in Los Angeles, took care of him. Remembering me as an anxious child, he told me not to worry about him, to enjoy my life, and to call him regularly, which I did, every day. He also asked me not to tell him what to do, as there were plenty of people around him who already did that. If he broke his neck, he said, it was *his* neck, after all. My father was not a perfect man, but he made sure, through his example, that we knew that our imperfections were forgivable—a lesson that has taken on more importance as I grow older. He never stopped providing me a path to follow.

When his death was imminent, his final wish was to die at home. Marie-Astrid and I drove south and waited in his Burbank condominium for his return from the hospital. It was getting late and he hadn't come, so we decided to head to Glendale to stay at my mother's house and visit in the morning. When he returned home near midnight, we were told that he gave a fist cheer upon his arrival and then died within a few hours. My father was a man who lived his life on his terms. That he should die the same way is as good as it gets.

My mother's health began to decline before the pandemic. Her dementia and anxiety, which increased with social isolation, were especially painful for an independent woman who prided herself on being a fighter and risk taker. During a visit to Los Angeles in June 2019, Marie-Astrid, Emiliano, Lucina, Fabiola, and I celebrated her birthday dinner at Las Golondrinas on Olvera Street, serenaded by a strolling duo. It was not easy to convince her to get out of her house, but once she heard the music, her spirits immediately lightened and she began to smile and engage in sustained conversations. For her birthday in 2020, I contracted the mariachi of Pepe Martínez Jr. to play for her on her front lawn. Although I could not be there in person, I saw videos, almost in real time, of my mother, who could hardly contain her joy, dancing and singing alongside the mariachi. In our daily phone calls afterward, she recited those memories, like a list, and they continued to bring her moments of lightness. For my mother's final birthday, in 2021, Marisol Hernandez kindly serenaded her with a trio, to which my mother sprang to life, temporarily becoming her youthful self. In November 2021, Marie-Astrid and I were finally able to visit my mother in her home, and I played guitar and sang for her myself. Music was the only activity that calmed her. She sang along and danced. Two months later, in January 2022, she died.

In 2022, as the most lethal days of the pandemic seemed to have waned, we began to welcome new students at our academy to join those who never left. We hired new staff members, all in their twenties and with a passion for tradition, archiving, and storytelling. Lucina, Fabiola, and I began to perform again as a trio, our most essential form. Verenice Velazquez joined us when possible, as did some of our teens, whose intensified training during those months of social distancing had solidified their deep, nuanced groove.

We returned to host our in-person Día de los Muertos event at our academy in November 2022. With support from our staff, faculty, students, and families, Marie-Astrid designed a remarkable, organic altar, which stood in the middle of our large hardwood floor. Our faculty and students performed chilenas from Oaxaca, sones from Jalisco and Veracruz, pirekuas from Michoacán, and huapangos from La Huasteca, all facing the altar, upon which we had placed ofrendas for those who had passed.

CHAPTER 17

•⬤•

REGENERATION

In 2012, the year I turned fifty, we recorded our thirtieth album, *Regeneration*. The songs were a colorful mix of traditional, popular, and original compositions played in a variety of styles that included regional Mexican music, Latin pop, psychedelic and old-school rock, and long instrumental jams. We even did a cover of Burt Bacharach's "Only Love Can Break a Heart," sung by Fabiola. Coproduced by David Hidalgo, the album featured old and new friends Jackson Browne, Elvin Bishop, Raul Malo, Pete Sears, Tom Fuglestad, Shira Kammen, Hector Espinoza, Cougar Estrada, and Carlos Caro. It was a pivotal year, as it was the last recording for which Hugo Arroyo and Emiliano Rodriguez appeared together before their departures from Los Cenzontles. Fourteen-year-old Verenice Velazquez graced the album cover wearing a dress hand embroidered by a contemporary designer and inspired by Mexican traditions.

Regeneration's themes and varied musical styles reflected on and celebrated America's transition toward a majority-minority society, as forecast by demographic trends. I thought that, four years into the two terms of our first African American president, it was the right time to celebrate cultural reconciliation with confidence, optimism, and gratitude. I was almost giddy imagining that our country could finally see itself as a Big We, in which everyone was mutually charged with shaping our society. I was convinced that the worst days of our country's racist menace were behind us, and that white supremacy was outnumbered and defeated. But I was wrong.

The tragedy of America's current rise of white supremacy not only caught me by surprise, but it has felt like a personal betrayal. I never would have thought that so many of my fellow Americans, including people with whom I grew up, could be so overtaken by petty racial resentment that they would betray their country and their neighbors. I long scoffed at the idea that our nation's history foretold the groundswell of white supremacy that was to come. But indeed it did, fully exposing the bald-faced lies and corruption that have always enabled racism. And this new chapter began with a predacious con man's denunciations of Mexicans as "rapists and murderers."

I grew up seeing my family story within America's arc of social progress, which I considered a sacred promise that justified the sacrifices and contributions made by people of color while enduring inequity. Both of my grandmothers became US citizens in their later years, filled with pride and gratitude. My Grandma Cacho routinely blessed us saying, "Dios los bendiga. God bless America." She understood that Mexico's cruel caste system would never have allowed her to escape the poverty within which she was born, whereas in this land of opportunity, her innate intelligence, ancestral faith, and work ethic enabled her and my grandfather to build bigger lives that economically

lifted up both them and subsequent generations of our family. She was, in my mind, the essence of this country's promise. Immigrants who come from corrupt societies value not just
America's economic opportunity but its system of justice, and
this has made the recent assault on our laws and norms not only
threatening to the very foundation of our country but also a
cruel mockery of those who have sacrificed for it.

When Los Cenzontles began in 1989, I had hoped to help
reinvigorate traditional cultural practices within the Mexican
American community; it was my contribution to our society, and
I wanted to do it not by promoting chauvinism, cultural brok-
ering, or identity litmus tests but by opening doors, dismantling
barriers, and promoting a decentralized vision of belonging.
Throughout the trajectory of Los Cenzontles, we have planted
many seeds, not only for us to harvest but as a benefit for everyone. My goal was never to suggest that our heritage was superior
but to simply show that it is no less valuable than any other, an
effort that is sadly still necessary when so many people, including some among ourselves, consider us to be inferior. I thought
that our work could help correct cultural misconceptions about
American identity that allow for our marginalization. To find
myself now at this painful moment in history, after a lifetime
struggling against bias, I have had to learn to recalibrate my
expectations. Today's loud, self-congratulatory declarations
against racism ring hollow to me, since "Latino" is not a racial
designation, a fact that few have the patience to acknowledge,
so our interests will continue to be overlooked. How can we
meaningfully remedy America's bias if we still do not even use
adequate language to discuss it? I can only hope that the arc of
social progress is simply much longer than I had thought, and
that future generations will continue to make progress.

Society's long-held beliefs about identity and belonging are
challenged by both recent and current mass global migrations of

people and their cultures. We are now as likely to find a master of regional Mexican folk music living in Mexico City or in the United States as we are to find them living in their place of origin. The rise of digital media has revealed Mexico's previously hidden traditions, but it has also made all of us more vulnerable to corporate manipulation. Artificial intelligence, meanwhile, simulates our deepest human functions and threatens to replace our ability to create with our hands and think with our minds, reducing us into a commodity. In response, the act of reclaiming our identity and sense of belonging becomes increasingly critical to the struggle to maintain human sovereignty.

The lifetimes of my parents, Manuel H. Rodriguez and Emilie Cacho, were different from mine, as each generation faces unique challenges and opportunities. They consciously forged paths upon which my brothers and I could travel a little easier, and I have tried to deepen their footprint for future generations to either follow or diverge from. Ultimately, it is not for any one generation to decide what the next will do; we must simply do our best to guide them as an act of faith and love. One of my life's biggest and most painful lessons was from our first child, Ariel, who died when he was only one month old. I realized, in time, that I grieved for who I hoped he would be, while, in fact, he had his own destiny. I had no choice but to accept that.

My father understood that, to truly be learned, he had to study not only the histories of America, Europe, and Mexico but also his family lineage, as well as his internal life—not to become stuck in a loop of introspection but to unlock and activate his potential to affect the world around him. I believe that woven into the intangible heritage that surrounds us are solutions and strategies within which we can find pathways toward revelation and freedom, however momentary. Resilience and hope are not things that can be bought or downloaded. They are embedded in the words, gestures, sounds, flavors, and images that connect us to ourselves and others. These are the traits that enabled our ancestors to persevere in times of war, poverty, and servitude. And I believe that they still can help guide us if we learn to value and trust the lessons of our own lives.

Our son Emiliano spent his childhood and young adulthood with us quietly observing the music and art making all around him, and then joining in when he felt ready. I once asked him about the difference between being backstage as a little boy and onstage as a teen. He replied that it was pretty much the same, as there was always something to do. He found ways to cultivate his interests, while Marie-Astrid and I supported and encouraged him. There is not much more we parents can do for our children than try to instill in them a sense of resourcefulness and resilience. Then it is up to them to find purpose, meaning, and joy on their own terms.

For our children, I wrote "Hijo Mío."

HIJO MÍO	MY SON
¿A donde vas?	Where are you going?
¿Y quien serás?	And who will you be?
Este mundo, tú sabrás	This world, you will know
No es tan fácil de andar	Is not as easy to navigate
Lo hallarás	You'll find it
Hijo mío	Oh my son
Lo hallarás	You will find it
¿De donde soy?	Where am I from?
¿Y a donde voy?	And where am I going?
Son preguntas que tendrás	These are questions you will have
Siempre conmigo contarás	You can always count on me
Lo hallarás	You'll find it
Hijo mío	Oh, my son
Lo hallarás	You will find it

Hijo mío	Oh, my son
Lo hallarás	You will find it
En la vida encontraras	In life you will find
Momentos de soledad	Moments of solitude
El miedo te engañará	Fear will deceive you
Y te da inseguridad	And make you feel uncertain
El tiempo es tan fugaz	Time is brief
Y no vuelve jamás	And it never returns
Nunca dejes de abrazar	Never stop embracing
El amor y la amistad	Love and friendship
Este mundo, tú sabrás	Life's path, you will see
No es tan fácil de andar	Is not always easy
Lo hallarás	You will find it
Hijo mío	Oh, my son
Lo hallarás	You'll find it
Hijo mío	Oh, my son
Lo hallarás	You'll find it
Hijo mío	Oh, my son
Lo hallarás	You will find it

For this book, I asked Angel Abundez, who began studying with me in 1987 at the age of ten, what Los Cenzontles provided him. He responded, "Los Cenzontles was everything for me growing up. I had what seemed like infinite experiences learning and playing music, singing, and dancing at every single stop. It gave me a tremendous sense of self-worth, confidence, and vision. All of the teachers and parents around me who were constantly encouraging me, cheering for me, and fighting for me gave me a sense that I had something in this world to contribute. It let me meet people, do things, and see parts of the world that I would never have experienced otherwise. I realized how much more there was all around me. Something bigger than myself. And that there was more to life. It's those same experiences I try to pass on to my children today. You're never quite sure what it is when you're a teenager, and you make mistakes along the way, but to be able to bounce back and keep moving forward, finding ways to persevere even when faced with adversity, requires a strong sense of purpose. This is what Cenzontles gave to me in my teen years. All young people deserve this, but many are not so lucky."

Reading what Angel wrote, I see that what I have tried to give my students was what my parents gave to me. For all our human advancements, the act of transmitting knowledge, skills, and support from person to person is still our most powerful tool. These many years later, I still find it thrilling to witness young people muster the confidence to risk expressing something newly found, filling a reservoir within them from which they can draw throughout their lives. And in those moments when they internalize knowledge, one can sense their spark, which jumps from person to person through generations, renewing an ancient flame that reaffirms and connects the best of our humanity. I see my work as nurturing the same spark within children that has provided shape and meaning to my life.

As a young person, I tried to understand how I fit into the world, and I always felt that I had something to contribute. But finding one's purpose in a society of distortion and bias is not a straight and easy path, just as finding simple, meaningful solutions is complicated. It was never my dream to become an executive director and fundraiser for a nonprofit organization. I have done these jobs because they were necessary to pursue and realize my vision. I never considered myself a singer, songwriter, producer, or author; I just had something to say and have found ways to say it. And though I have been inventive, I have invented nothing. I am merely passing along, as best I can, what has been passed on to me.

Through all of my struggles and losses, which can feel crushing at the end of a day, I have, so far, managed to keep waking up the next day with enough strength to continue seeking a path forward. In a world where being oneself can be treacherous, I am most grateful that, in my search, I have been able to employ the fullness of who I am and where I come from. This is resilience, my ancestral inheritance, a strength that I have tried to nurture in others. It is the most powerful force in life, much like the power that allows wildflowers to break through the cement of our neighborhood sidewalks and reach toward the sky.

ACKNOWLEDGMENTS

I could not possibly list all of the people who contributed to this book, which itself is an acknowledgment to them and many others. So, I will limit my thanks here to the people who assisted and encouraged me as I wrote it and helped to make its publication possible.

Thank you to: Judy Bernhard and Byron Spooner for holding my hand throughout; Norma Cantú, Lawrence Downes, and Tamara Johnston for their learned encouragement; James Hall for working so thoughtfully with every iteration of this book while preparing it for film; Frances Phillips and Verenice Velazquez for their help as this story found its voice; Charlotte Sheedy for suggesting this become a memoir; Joel Selvin for providing a cinematic metaphor that helped me add dimension; Dave Millar and Barbara Selhorst for so often suggesting the better word; Lisa K. Marietta for her extraordinary insights on language and clarity; Daniel Handler for his warm and joyful support and faith; Marie-Astrid for empathizing with my cathartic process of memory recall; MJ Bogatin for his wise counsel; Richard Rodriguez for lighting the path; and Steve Wasserman and Heyday for bringing my story to the world.

ABOUT THE AUTHOR

Eugene Rodriguez is the founder and executive director of Los Cenzontles Cultural Arts Academy, a nonprofit based in San Pablo, California. Since forming Los Cenzontles in 1989, Rodriguez has produced more than thirty albums and numerous films for the organization, and he has collaborated with Linda Ronstadt, Jackson Browne, Los Lobos, Lalo Guerrero, Ry Cooder, the Chieftains, and Taj Mahal, among others. His work has been featured in the *New York Times*, the *Los Angeles Times*, the *San Francisco Chronicle*, and NPR. He is also the recipient of several awards and fellowships, including from the California Arts Council and United States Artists. He lives in Richmond, California.

A NOTE ON TYPE

The main text of this book is set in Adobe Garamond Pro. Garamond, created by Claude Garamond in the sixteenth century and reinterpreted for digital use by Robert Slimbach and Adobe, is one of the most widely praised typefaces in design history, noted for its exceptional elegance and readability.

The chapter titles are set in Holtwood One SC, designed by Vernon Adams and inspired by nineteenth-century woodblock posters. The chapter numbers are set in Phosphate, which was designed by Steve Jackaman and Ashley Muir and published by the Red Rooster Collection.